MW00435904

Walking

Towards

Pentecost

by Anne Neufeld Rupp

WALKING TOWARDS PENTECOST
by Anne Neufeld Rupp

copyright © 1996 Anne Neufeld Rupp

Printed in the United States of America. All rights reserved. Portions may be reproduced for church use only.

ISBN 1-877871-95-8

Educational Ministries, Inc.

165 Plaza Drive

Prescott, AZ 86303

800-221-0910

CONTENTS

INTRODUCTION

WHY AN EASTER TO PENTECOST EMPHASIS?

Pentecost is the climax of the church year. It follows the waiting of Advent, the good news of the Incarnation, the sorrow of Lent, the agony of the Passion and the joy of the Resurrection. Yet for many members of our congregations, Pentecost is dissociated from the rest of the church year, and appears to be less important than Christmas, Easter, Advent or Lent. We have only to look at how we prepare for each major church holiday. During Advent we spend four Sundays moving towards Christmas. Before Easter we prepare for Good Friday, with five weeks of Lent. The week preceding Easter contains a mixture of celebration and sorrow. During those last days, we hail Jesus' entrance into Jerusalem, quietly partake in the Lord's supper on Maundy Thursday, and bow with grief when we think of the tortured death of the Messiah on Good Friday.

In the church, we participate in observances leading towards Christmas and Easter, each one culminating in the festivities connected with it. These observances are like scenes in an act, each contributing to the rising action in a larger drama. But because Easter is often regarded as the climax of God's mighty acts in our midst, the post-resurrection events that follow, become disconnected responses to the resurrection. Pentecost becomes an epilogue. Why this separation?

The first reason for the separation may occur because we don't appreciate the meaning of Pentecost. Pentecost, is God's miraculous and mystifying act of birthing the church. If it assumes its rightful place, Pentecost, rather than Easter, becomes the climax of the drama, and the high point of the church year. Then the post Easter events dramatize scenes in an intense act, that propel us towards Pentecost. A drama so great, it continues to be written and rewritten in the life of each believer and congregation. We then are part of the climax, rather than falling action of this drama. That realization empowers and enlivens our view of the church's purpose and mission today.

The second reason for the separation may occur because we don't acknowledge the significance of the Holy Spirit. Pentecost is proclaimed as the day on which the Spirit appeared to a gathered few, and historically affirmed an event which spurred the church into full blown existence. Yet for some, the Holy Spirit is little more than a ghostly apparition, a charismatic experience or a personal comforter. Many of the Holy Spirit hymns we sing, seem rather passive. Years ago, through study and reflection, I woke to the fact that the Holy Spirit came with power and fire, not only gentle wings of compassion and guidance. In the original Greek, the word power is 'dunamais,' the root of our explosive word, 'dynamite.' Shortly thereafter I wrote the Pentecost hymn, "Holy Spirit, Come With Power," <u>Hymnal: A Worship Book</u>. Elgin, IL: Brethren Press; Newton, KS: Faith and Life Press; Scottdale, PA: Mennonite Publishing House, 1992, #26.

One of the reasons for an Easter to Pentecost emphasis, is to help our congregations understand that the Holy Spirit is much more than glossolalia or personal experience. The Holy Spirit is that aspect of the Trinity, already present at creation (Genesis 1:2), who represents God at work in the world, in our congregations, and in our lives. In a time where the voice and authority of the church's message appears to weaken in the face of our nation's preoccupation with its social, economic or political troubles—in a time of increasing secularization and attempts to look for deliverance elsewhere than in the divine, the church needs to speak with a fresh voice and a renewed conviction. The Holy Spirit is the driving force behind each congregation. The extent to which a congregation opens itself to that catalyst, determines whether that group will live or die, whether it will be dynamite or routine ritual, whether it will share good news or hide its head in the sand.

What happens when we begin to view the Holy Spirit as power? The book of Acts demonstrates proof and consequence of those who accepted and affirmed this holy force. In the early church this 'dynamite' was evidenced through new found courage and zeal. That courage to change, to look at new possibilities and options, evoked the realization that God's power through the Holy Spirit, could break down all walls of prejudice, discrimination and ostracism.

There is nothing boring or passive about the Holy Spirit. Here lies a power that defies traditional thinking and the limitations of social, ethnic or racial boundaries. It turns ordinary people like the apostle Peter, Paul, you and I, into powerballs. It confronts God's people with surprises and elements of the unexpected. The Holy Spirit has a way of turning the world upside down.

HOW TO USE THIS BOOK

Churches are diverse. The sizes of congregation vary. Worship and education differ from one local setting to another. Programs planned in each local setting differ. Walking Towards Pentecost contains several sections. You may select those that best meet the needs of the adults, youth and children in your congregation. It is written in such a way that you may adapt and change any part of the material without impeding the flow that moves the local congregation from Easter to Pentecost. Most of the topics for the eight Sundays are similar, but the themes may vary. Although written in three parts, many of these divisions are interchangeable. You may borrow from one and adapt to another. This gives you the flexibility to plan around the size of your congregation and the ages in it.

I believe that in an era of diversity and numerous congregational needs, it is the task and calling of pastors and educators, to empower all ages in the church for worship, education and mission. Because the Christian faith is a way of life, not dogma, we must explore all possible avenues and ways for the good news to be reborn, and come alive for individuals. Christian discipleship is then an exciting adventure, filled with joy and anticipation. Joy is always at the center of the good news.

Budget often limits a church's ability to invest in materials that meet a number of needs. Walking Towards Pentecost, attempts to overcome that limitation by providing resources and ideas for different settings, different needs, and different ages, all on one package. It is divided in the following way.

Part I—THE CONGREGATION AT WORSHIP

In Walking Towards Pentecost, the congregation at worship experiences the week by week joy, hope and excitement of the Jesus appearances. These unexpected, (sometimes unusual) disclosures by Jesus, move steadily towards a climax, the revelation of the Holy Spirit on Pentecost Sunday. The ecstatic mood throughout is not unlike that of the earlier Nativity narratives. The joy of the post resurrection events however, is expressed by more people and experienced by a greater number of followers (1 Corinthians 15:5-6). In comparison, the jubilant few who witnessed to the birth of Christ, are indeed but a few.

These weekly themes come alive for the congregation through the use of the suggested resources. No two Sundays use the same approach. In the material you will find hymn suggestions, ideas for skits, responsive readings, prayers, Reader's Theater, sermon themes and various other options. Suggestions for bulletin covers, direct involvement of all ages in some aspect of the service, and an insert for family activities are also included.

Part II—CHILDREN WORSHIP AND LEARN

The elementary grades meet for a brief assembly before dispersing to their classes. The worship experience, expresses the theme, and presents the story in skit form. Teachers enact the skits and lead the session. A theme song, visuals, direct participation and many other forms of worship, help the stories come alive for the children. Following the assembly, the children meet in three age groups, Preschool-Kindergarten, Primary and Junior. The theme is now developed in age appropriate ways, with a strong emphasis on involvement and direct participation. The series closes with a Birth of the Church Party, on the eighth Sunday, Pentecost morning.

Part III—INTERGENERATIONAL WORSHIP AND ACTIVITY

During the Church School hour, all ages meet for a short time of input and worship. The stated theme uses skits, songs and other direct participation to bring the story to life. The script for the skits is written out. It may be presented with minimal rehearsal. Attempts are made to involve adults, youth and children in these skits, or some part of the worship experience. By meeting together, all generations gather in a celebrative setting. By worshiping together, an intergenerational bonding between generations occurs. This is especially helpful if parents and their children are involved.

During the second part of this gathering, all ages congregate in the Fellowship Hall for activities, hands-on experiences and refreshments. Suggestions, patterns and procedures are described and listed in the resources. Adults and youth may choose to participate in a related study group. On the eighth Sunday, Pentecost, all ages celebrate a Pentecost Party, adding another dimension to the intergenerational experience.

It is assumed that your congregation at worship will meet at its regular time. You will need to adapt Part II or III accordingly, depending on whether the worship service precedes or follows your education hour. In the event that it precedes the Church School hour, and you are using Part III, you may choose to move directly into the intergenerational and refreshment time in the Fellowship Hall, and then move to an assembly setting.

Part I

THE CONGREGATION AT WORSHIP

A number of years ago, members of a Worship Committee in a large, General Conference Mennonite Church, where my husband and I served as pastors, enriched the life of the congregation with creative, participatory approaches to worship. One year, I presented the Lenten Easter themes for their consideration and feedback. I assumed they would come up with some creative worship ideas as they had earlier. But Pentecost was at work.

"How come we focus on Lent?" asked a member. "Aren't we post- resurrection people? Why aren't we emphasizing what happened after Easter?"

The discussion that followed brought new perspectives and observations to both committee members and myself. I laid my carefully planned Lenten themes aside, and we proceeded to discuss Easter to Pentecost. The themes in this worship section and much of what you find here, is the story of what our committee did. Some adaptations have been made, songs and other resources have been added. Some bulletin cover ideas have been added. The Pentecost Wreath is new to this material.

Not only the worship resources are based on this earlier experience. The architecture of the sanctuary is also similar. The setting for the service assumes three aisles, a U shaped balcony, a large stage with only a center pulpit, and a choir loft behind the pulpit. Awareness of the interior design of a sanctuary helps you visualize changes and adaptations you will need to make.

THE CONGREGATION AT WORSHIP consists of three major parts:

A. THE DRAMA OF WORSHIP follows the expressed theme. In this skit or vignette using dialogue, music and response, individuals enact some aspect of the post-resurrection event. It blends into the remaining part of the worship service. To maintain an element of surprise, similar to that of the early disciples, the drama doesn't appear at the same place in the service each Sunday, nor is it presented in the same style. The highlight of this series is the Pentecost Banner which is begun at Easter and hung Pentecost morning by a group of parading children.

B. RESOURCES FOR THE SERVICE OF WORSHIP features the Pentecost Wreath and intergenerational candle lighting services. Also included are weekly ideas for bulletin covers, some which may be copied or adapted for your use. Numerous other resources are included. You will find Invocations using different approaches—songs, poems and sections of the Lord's Prayer. Two types of Readers' Theater are included. In addition to this, varied Calls to Worship and prayers as well as songs by the author, help enrich the service.

C. EMPOWERING THE FAMILY. Based on the belief that the role of the church includes strengthening its families at all levels, this section is a bulletin insert, which may be used as is, or adapted for your congregation. It attempts to relate to the weekly theme. It provides opportunity for families or extended families of the church to gather, discuss, share and grow through their communal experience. It may be used as in insert, as part of a family life publication, or enlarged on a full page to make it more readable for children. Enhancing it with visuals will make it more 'user friendly.'

Easter Sunday

On The Third Day Rise

John 20:11-18

THEME HYMN: "Holy Spirit, Come With Power." Hymnal: A Worship Book. Elgin, IL: Brethren Press; Newton, KS: Faith and Life Press; Scottdale, PA: Mennonite Publishing House, 1992, #26 (or EXHIBIT A-1).

THEME: Joy permeates the gospel; from Incarnation, (through life and ministry of Jesus), to Resurrection, Ascension to Pentecost (through life and ministry of the emerging church), then and now.

A. THE DRAMA OF WORSHIP

A Call To Worship: No Prelude on Easter morning. Committee members, contact a local garden center, which may provide trees, plants and shrubs, to create a pastoral setting. (Consider alternatives such as a collection of houseplants.)

Make a large, styrofoam tombstone, spray with gray paint and set it near the back of the garden. Mary, costumed, enters through the choir loft and walks slowly down the stairs. While walking, she sadly sings, "Woman's Lament," (EXHIBIT A-2) without accompaniment. She stands in a weeping position. Jesus, in costume, enters on the other side of the choir loft and quietly walks down the stairs. He stands behind Mary. The recognition scene from John 20:11-18 is acted out. As Mary falls on her knees in adoration, the organ and congregation burst forth with the jubilant, "Christ the Lord is Risen Today." During the singing, Mary hurries down a side aisle, to share the good news. Jesus slowly exits down center aisle.

Alternate hymn selections

"Lift Your Glad Voices" Hymnal: A Worship Book. Elgin, IL: Brethren Press; Newton, KS: Faith and Life Press; Scottdale, PA: Mennonite Publishing House, 1982, #275.

"Allelu!" Workers Quarterly, Hymns for Now. Chicago, IL: Walther League, July 1967, #5.

B. RESOURCES FOR THE SERVICE OF WORSHIP

Lighting the Pentecost Wreath *(see Exhibit A-6)*

Family or extended family comes forward.

Adult/Youth 1:	*Reads John 11:25.*
Older Child:	*Reads Matthew 28:5-6, 8.*
Child 1:	*Lights white candle, #1.*
Child 2:	"Why do we light this first candle?"
Adult/Youth 2:	"This candle reminds us of **HOPE** and **JOY.** Jesus Christ, born in Bethlehem and crucified at Golgatha, has risen. Jesus lives. That is our joy. We too shall live eternally. That is our hope. Hope and joy."

The Bulletin Cover

Several weeks in advance, suggest all ages hand in two-inch squares of paper on which they depict the joy and hope of Easter. Select a number of these and create a collage. Superimpose lettering, where words are required.

A Benediction

A benediction is the blessing and the final sending forth of God's people. It may take various shapes from the traditional Numbers 6:24-26, to selections from Paul's epistles, hymns or hymn words, benedictions written by the pastor or members of the congregation, or those that mix many of the foregoing. The following responsive benediction focuses on the joy theme, emphasized throughout this Easter-Pentecost series.

Pastor:	Go! Tell it on the mountains, over the hills and everywhere!
Congregation:	What shall we tell, from the mountaintops and hills, What shall we sing to this crowded, circling earth?
Pastor:	Tell them the Good News still lives; all is well, Declare that death has been canceled, once and for all. Shout aloud the message of joy and hope, "Jesus is risen!"
Congregation:	Alleluia! Alleluia! We go forth as Easter people!

The Pentecost Banner

Appoint Banner Makers to do the following: Purchase cream colored material for two long banners. Lay the banners on tables in the narthex. All ages cut flames from various colors and prints of cloth (*a pattern may be made available for those who want it*) at home. Each Sunday they bring flames to church and lay them on the banner. The Banner Makers adhere the flames to the banner at lower midpoint, creating a huge, colorful fire. During the last week, the Banner Makers cut two white, descending doves and glue one above the flames on each banner. They also cut red lettering with words such as, HOLY SPIRIT COME! or GOD'S SPIRIT IS HERE! Paint dowels red or cream and insert. Attach cord.

The banners will be hung by the elementary grades on Pentecost morning. (*See Eighth Sunday*) Plan how and where they will be hung. The way banners are hung, depends on the size and architecture of the sanctuary. A long stick with a hook at the end may suffice, if a small stepladder doesn't. For high ceilings and long banners, attach a pulley to the fastener on the wall and lead a long cord through it. Tie a hook at one end and a loop at the other. A child attaches the banner to the hook and others pull the cord until it is raised. Attach the loop to a hook below to keep the banner from slipping.

Planning Ahead

Ask a a soloist and choir or octet to learn the theme song, "Holy Spirit, Come With Power." Hymnal: A Worship Book. Elgin IL: Brethren Press; Newton, KS: Faith and Life Press; Scottdale, PA: Mennonite Publishing House, 1992, #26 (or EXHIBIT A-1)

C. EMPOWERING THE FAMILY:

(*A bulletin insert for each week.*)

**Families Celebrate 50 Days,
Easter to Pentecost:**

Celebrate the resurrection with this song. Simple words and melody, make it easy to learn and sing. You may wish to use it for a table grace today. Add your own words and use it throughout the Easter-Pentecost season.

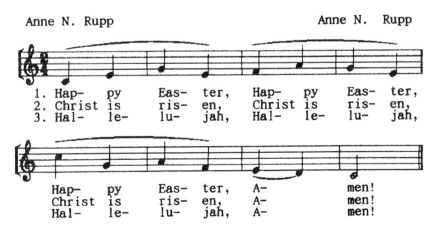

HAPPY EASTER

Anne N. Rupp   Anne N. Rupp

1. Hap- py Eas- ter, Hap- py Eas- ter,
2. Christ is ris- en, Christ is ris- en,
3. Hal- le- lu- jah, Hal- le- lu- jah,

Hap- py Eas- ter, A- men!
Christ is ris- en, A- men!
Hal- le- lu- jah, A- men!

STAY WITH US

Luke 24:13-29

THEME: Hospitality is an essential ingredient of the Christian faith (Romans 12;13). An open home may be evidence of an open heart.

A. THE DRAMA OF WORSHIP

The Invocation: Following the Call to Worship and Hymn of Praise, two in costume, walk down the center aisle in a slow, measured pace. They re-enact the Luke 24:13-29 incident. They discuss the events of the week and express grief over the loss of the Master. Their concern is that the root of Jesse, whom they thought to be the Messiah, is now dead. The Kingdom of Israel (*which the apostles later inquire about, Acts 1:6*) now has no leader. Now what? While the discussion continues, Jesus enters, follows them and soon overtakes them. He joins them and enters the conversation. He discusses the fulfillment of prophecy, referring to parables he told earlier. As the dynamics of this conversation intensify, all three arrive near the front of the sanctuary. The two beg Jesus to come and stay with them. Jesus agrees. They exit through a side door. The congregation responds with a unison Invocation. While heads are bowed, a soloist sings stanza 1 of the theme hymn, "Holy Spirit, Come With Power." (EXHIBIT A-1)

B. RESOURCES FOR THE SERVICE OF WORSHIP

Lighting the Pentecost Wreath

A family or extended family comes forward.

Adult/Youth 1:	*Lights candle 1. Reads Hebrews 13:2.*
Older Child:	*Reads Luke 24:28-29.*
Child 1:	*Lights white candle #2.*
Child 2:	"Why do we light this second candle?"
Adult/Youth 2:	This candle reminds us of **SHARING**. Whenever we give of ourselves, share what we have, and open our homes to others, Jesus is there."

The Bulletin Cover

Invite an adult in the church to design a bulletin cover, based on the theme and scripture. Or use this one (*designed by Fern Bartel, member of the Alexanderwohl Mennonite Church, Goessel, KS*)

"Stay with us....." Luke 24:29

Unison Invocation

The Invocation serves as an invitation and appears near the beginning of the worship hour. It may be spoken by the pastor or by the congregation in unison or as responsive reading. The invocation may also be a hymn or a stanza of a hymn, sung by the congregation. Often a choir, soloist or group may sing the invocation. The following unison invocation may be spoken by the congregation, a group of youth or older children.

> Stay with us Lord Jesus,
> We need you every day.
> Be our strength and comforter,
> Guide us on our way.
>
> Stay with us Lord Jesus,
> We need you every hour.
> Be our Lord and Master,
> Guide us with your power.
>
> Stay with us Lord Jesus,
> Morning, noon and night.
> Be our wisdom, truth and way,
> Guide us with your light. Amen.

Planning Ahead

If the children are participating in Part II or III of this book, they will know the song, "It's Jesus Christ, Hallelujah!" (EXHIBIT A-3). If not, ask teachers to help them learn it. Children may lead out in singing stanzas on pending Sundays.

C. EMPOWERING THE FAMILY:

Families Celebrate 50 Days, Easter to Pentecost:

On this first Sunday after Easter, take time to think, reflect and talk about Jesus. Here are some talk-starters your family may want to use. If you have younger children, make these talk-times age appropriate. Think of pictures you could use or a game you could make up.

TALK-STARTER: Here are some words for you to think and talk about. Which of these words best describe what Jesus is like for you:

- kind
- friendly
- forgiving
- strong
- love
- serious
- fun
- gentle

Fill in other words here _____

THEIR EYES WERE OPENED

Luke 24:30-33a

THEME: The early church recognized the Christ in the shared fellowship and breaking of bread together. Christ continues to come to us in the ordinary events of our daily lives.

A. THE DRAMA OF WORSHIP:

Present this theme in two parts, one at the beginning and the other at the end of the service.

The Invocation in Song and Word: Place a large, round loaf of bread on the communion table. Following the Prelude, a group or duet sings stanza 2 of "Holy Spirit, Come With Power." (EXHIBIT A-1) During the last phrase, Jesus and the two from Emmaus enter, using the same door through which they exited the previous Sunday. They stop beside the communion table. Cleopas, the host, welcomes Jesus as guest. Jesus takes the bread, blesses it, and speaks the Lord's Prayer as Invocation beginning with, "Give us this day....." (*The two and congregation may join in.*) The disciples, awed, recognize him and cry out, "Jesus!" They freeze in this pose. Children or a children' choir respond with stanza 1 of, "It's Jesus Christ, Hallelujah." (EXHIBIT A-3) During the song, Jesus, leaves as he came and the disciples exit down center aisle. Their walk and facial expressions exude the joy they feel.

This theme provides opportunity for the celebration of the Lord's Supper (Holy Communion).

The Departing: Place a low table and a chair near the pulpit, before the worship service begins. Set an unlit candle on the table. Before the end of the worship service the congregation sings a departing hymn, "Bless'd Be the Tie that Binds." During the singing a costumed disciple enters, sits down at the table and lights the candle. Other disciples come in through various doors and some directly out of the congregation. Their furtive actions and facial expressions show their fear. The two from Emmaus hurry in and pantomime what they have seen. As the hymn ends, Jesus appears. The actions and responses show the joy of the disciples as they cry out, "It is the Lord!" One disciple moves closer, holds out his hands and begs, "Be with us, Lord Jesus! They keep this pose, while the pastor speaks the Benediction. The congregation responds by singing, an appropriate benediction hymn such as "May the Grace of Christ our Savior" The Mennonite Hymnal, Scottdale, PA: Herald Press; Newton, KS: Faith and Life Press, 1970 #647. The pastor walks down center aisle, followed by the disciples.

B. RESOURCES FOR WORSHIP

Lighting the Pentecost Wreath

A family or extended family comes forward.

Adult/Youth 1:	*Lights candles 1-2. Reads John 14:1.*
Older Child:	*Read John 14:19b-20.*
Child 1:	*Lights white candle #3.*
Child 2:	"Why do we light this third candle?"
Adult/Youth 2:	"This candle reminds us of **TRUST.** Wherever we are, wherever we go, whatever happens, Jesus is with us. We need not be afraid."

The Bulletin Cover

Ask a photographer in the congregation to take a picture of a loaf of bread or a group of people eating together.

The Lord's Prayer as Invocation

The Lord's Prayer is often used as a part of the pastoral or congregational prayer. It is the model for prayer taught by Jesus, and needs to be an important part of congregational life and worship. Frequent repetition of the prayer may keep the congregation from thinking about the full meaning. Using segments of it in other parts of the service, provides another dimension to worship. The first part may be used for a call to worship. The second part may be used as an invocation. It could also be made into a litany or antiphonal prayer.

C. EMPOWERING THE FAMILY

Families Celebrate 50 Days, Easter to Pentecost:

This week, invite someone for a meal or dessert who has never been in your home before. Invite those whose experiences are different from yours, job or career-wise. Consider those whose status or lifestyle is different from yours. If you are single, invite a family. If you are elderly, invite a single parent family. If you have children at home, invite someone who has no children. The church is a community of Christ, regardless of age, gender, race or marital status.

UNLESS I SEE

John 20:19-29

THEME: Apart from the Matthew resurrection account, none of Jesus' disciples believed in his resurrection until he appeared to them. The Thomas story raises faith to another level; faith that seeks confirmation must be superseded by faith and trust that hold fast when no proof is evident. Faith is an outrageous risk.

A. THE DRAMA OF WORSHIP:

A Contemporary Scripture Presentation: After the scripture reading from John 20:19-29, a group sings stanza 3 of "Holy Spirit, Come With Power." (EXHIBIT A-1) Follow this with a contemporary scripture presentation based on the earlier reading. Instead of improvising, plan, write and memorize the script.

This reading requires several participants, including some of the disciples who were a part of earlier presentations. The group may use the dialogue from Part III, Fourth Sunday, as a basic outline and put it into a 20th or 21st century setting, or write and shape it after study of the text.

The children or children's choir move into place, ready to sing. Disciples walk on stage, talking to each other. Thomas who hasn't seen the Lord, stands to one side. The disciples converse with him, trying to allay his doubts. Thomas, a computer analyst, wants a computer printout of data, or concise information from the Internet. Or he wants to hear a news report from a major network. Or failing all else, the least he will settle for is a video of the appearance. *Keep the theme in mind, as the disciples encourage faith during disaster, suffering and even during affluent living—times when the Divine appears either absent, obsolete or even unnecessary. God not only waits on us to respond (Luke 15:20) but also pursues us (Revelation 3:20). Faith is God's gift.*

A contemporary Jesus enters and invites Thomas to become a believer. He commends Thomas for a head faith and encourages him to integrate knowledge and perception with a heart faith. The new insight and understanding change Thomas. The group steps back as he moves forward in awe and falls on his knees before Jesus. Freeze. A children's choir sings stanzas 1-2, 4-5, "It's Jesus Christ, Hallelujah!" (EXHIBIT A-3) Jesus invites all disciples to join him in the upper room. Together they walk up the stairs of the choir loft and exit.

B. RESOURCES FOR THE SERVICE OF WORSHIP

Lighting the Pentecost Wreath

A family or extended family comes forward.

Adult/Youth 1:	*Lights candles 1-3. Reads Hebrews 11:1.*
Older Child:	*Reads John 20: 28-29.*
Child 1:	*Lights pink candle, #4.*
Child 2:	"Why do we light this fourth candle?"
Adult/Youth 2:	"This candle reminds us of **FAITH**. We can believe in a resurrected Jesus, who is the Way, the Truth and the Life. We cannot see him, but we are assured he is with us."

The Bulletin Cover

Ask a group or individual to design a symbol for faith or use historical symbols of the church. Or use this one depicting various stages of faith.

"If you have faith
as a grain of mustard
seed....." Matthew 17:20

A Call to Worship in Word

A call to worship is exactly that. It calls the gathered community to worship, to focus on the great, everlasting, ever-present God. A call to worship may be sung, spoken by the pastor or read responsively. The following call to worship in word, focuses on the greatness of God, revealed to us through Jesus Christ.

Pastor:	Blessed be the God and Father of our Lord Jesus Christ; By great mercy we have been born anew To a living hope, Through the resurrection of Jesus Christ From the dead.
Congregation:	We have an inheritance which is imperishable. Undefiled and unfading.
Pastor:	Sing praises to the Lord Who is highly exalted.
Congregation:	Sing for joy, O heavens,

And exult, O earth.
For the Lord has brought joy to all people.

Pastor: Hallelujah! For the Lord God reigns
And shall reign forever and ever.

All: Thanks be to the God of gods,
Praise be to the Lord of lords.

C. EMPOWERING THE FAMILY:

Families Celebrate 50 Days, Easter to Pentecost:

MAKE A FAITH SHIELD.

This week, take time as a family, to talk about faith. What do you believe about God, Jesus, the Holy Spirit, prayer, peace, the church? Below is a pattern for a 'Family Faith Shield.' Enlarge it and make copies (*or family members draw their own*). In the six spaces, write about (*or draw*) some of your beliefs. Or list ways you have acted out what you believe. Or make a sketch about how God has answered your prayers.

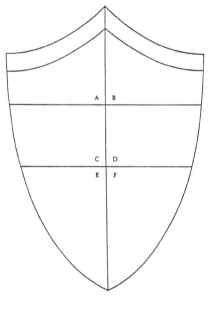

If there are children in your family, they may want to color the spaces. Hang your shields on the wall for family members to see during the remaining days and weeks before Pentecost. If a guest or friend asks, "What is this?" you have an opportunity to share your faith.

COME AND HAVE BREAKFAST

John 21:1-14

THEME: The gospels resound with joy and invitation. Jesus invites followers to participate in his life, and through fellowship be empowered to take on the demands of discipleship. Jesus initiates the communing invitation to come and dine with him (Revelation 3:20), and the commitment invitation to take up the cross and follow Mark 8:34-36. That initiative makes response possible.

A. THE DRAMA OF WORSHIP

The Sharing Community: Education and worship may be integrated through a fellowship time that focuses on the morning's theme. Both Church School and the Service of Worship need to be cut by half an hour. This gives a full hour for fellowship, sharing and eating together. (*Less time is required if your congregation is small.*)

Make and hang a long paper banner over a table in the fellowship hall. The focal point of the banner is a large sketch, based on the line drawing style in the Good News Bible (TEV). It shows Jesus standing on the shore and calling out to the fishermen. Under the drawing, inscribe in large lettering, "Come and Have Breakfast." Serve juice, rolls and coffee.

If your worship service is first, plan it in such a way that the message, scripture reading or prayer will not be interrupted. Anticipate, that after 30 minutes, the disciples will enter, dressed in rough, homespun robes and sandals. They come to the front, beckon the worshipers and call out, "Come and have breakfast." The disciples hold that pose as the pastor asks all to rise. He or she speaks a thanksgiving-benediction prayer. The pastor and disciples lead the way to the fellowship hall, and worshipers follow.

If Church School is first, adults and youth (disciples) dressed in rough hemp-like robes and sandals, spread through the building after classes have met for almost half an hour. They knock at and open classroom doors, and call out, "Come and have breakfast." All ages move to the fellowship hall to celebrate the invitation. Following the time of eating and sharing, the pastor speaks a prayer of thanksgiving. All move to the sanctuary for a short worship service. Don't follow the usual order of service but make the time of worship reflective and meditative. Sing stanzas 1-2 and 5 from, "It's Jesus Christ, Hallelujah! (EXHBIT A-3) for a Call to Worship. Integrate the morning's experience with the meaning of Jesus' invitation for us today. An alternative to a half hour regular service is a hymn, prayer, brief homily and the celebration of the Lord's Supper (*Holy Communion*).

B. RESOURCES FOR THE SERVICE OF WORSHIP

Lighting the Pentecost Wreath

A family or extended family comes forward.

Adult/Youth:	*Lights candles 1-4. Reads John 15:12-14.*
Older Child:	*Reads John 21:12-13.*
Child 1:	*Lights pink candle, #5.*
Child 2:	"Why do we light this fifth candle?"
Adult/Youth 2:	"This candle reminds us of **RELATIONSHIPS**. Jesus has shown us that being his follower means being friends, Jesus' friends and friends with each other."

The Bulletin Cover

Make a replica of the banner used during the fellowship meal. Children's classes may want to color these bulletins.

The Closing Prayer

The closing prayer contains an element of a sending forth to live the Christ-like life. It also contains invocation for the journey ahead, petition for the strength and wisdom to find one's way, and a commitment to walk the narrow path. The following unison prayer takes into consideration both the aspects of being fed and going forth to share the abundant life.

> Send us forth, Master
> As those convinced of life worth living,
> As those committed to open handed
> self-giving,
> As those wanting shared wholeness.
> Let us be light
>   salt
>   bread
> In a dark, tasteless, hungry world.
> Hallelujah. Amen.

C. EMPOWERING THE FAMILY

Families Celebrate 50 Days, Easter to Pentecost

This week, we think about the disciples. What it meant for them to meet Jesus in Galilee, and have breakfast with him. As a part of our worship service this morning, we came together for rolls and drink. Jesus invites us, as he did the disciples, to come and have breakfast, to fellowship with him and with each other.

The disciples were fishing, when Jesus appeared to them. Plan to have a fish supper with your family this week. Set an extra plate and chair for an unexpected guest, or a reminder of Jesus' presence.

"Lo, I am with you always...." Matthew 28:20

FEED MY LAMBS.

John 21:15-19

THEME: Nurturing the children and youth of the church through worship, education, and participation, builds a strong faith community. It is equaled only by the church's task of educating adults; strengthening them to live by faith, and empowering parents to nurture the faith of their children. Both lambs and sheep must be fed.

A. THE DRAMA OF WORSHIP

Song, Story and Sermon: This theme provides opportunity for Child Dedication (*Infant Baptism*). Depending on when Easter occurs, it may fall on the traditional Mother's Day Sunday (*Festival of the Christian Home*). The Committee works closely with the pastor to help shape a service of song, story and sermon.

Song: The Holy Spirit is the empowering force of the church and needed for wisdom and guidance in the nurture of it's children. The Invocation, "Holy Spirit, Come with Power," (EXHIBIT A-1) is sung by the choir or congregation. The worshipers sing several children's hymns. A soloist sings, "I Am Jesus' Little Lamb," (EXHIBIT A-4) as parents bring their children forward for the dedication (*or baptism*). Sing stanza 7 of, "It's Jesus Christ, Hallelujah," (EXHIBIT A-3) as a benediction response.

Story: Place an emphasis on story in the service. Parents or grandparents may share brief vignettes of faith stories related to childhood experiences, or times with their children. The sermon may include various stories. Include a "Time for Children" and tell, A "Lamb's Tale." The storyteller walks down center aisle, carrying a live lamb. The children follow. They sit around the storyteller. Encourage them to pet the lamb while the story is shared.

Sermon: Story is a strong medium for communicating the message.

1. *Illustrative Sermon:* Use stories and illustrate with visuals.

2. *Story Sermon:* Tell a story dramatically. Use gestures, facial expressions and other body language. Enhance with music background.

3. *Dramatic Monologue:* This format in free verse or story form, is a first person account. Appear in the costume of the disciple, Peter. Share your perceptions about the importance of the Christian home and the faith nurture of children. Consider thoughts about child nurture found in the Bible: Deuteronomy 6:4-9, Joshua 4;20-24, Psalms 78:1-7, Matthew 18:1-6, 19;13-14, Mark 10:13-16, Luke 18:15-17, Ephesians 6:4. Incorporate Peter's experience in John 21:15. Begin with, "My name is Peter," and take it from there.

B. RESOURCES FOR THE SERVICE OF WORSHIP

Lighting the Pentecost wreath

A family or extended family comes forward.

Adult/Youth 1:	*Lights candles 1-5. Reads Romans 5:8.*
Older Child:	*Reads John 21:15.*
Child 1:	*Lights pink candle, #6.*
Child 2:	"Why do we light this sixth candle?"
Adult/Youth 2:	"This candle reminds us of **LOVE**. God's great love for us, our love for Jesus and for others."

The Bulletin Cover

Ask several youth to design a bulletin cover, based on John 21:15-19. Or use something like this one.

Feed my lambs....
Tend my sheep....
Feed my sheep....
John 21:15-16

A Story

Including senses in story telling enhances learning and memory. In this story, most of the children's senses are incorporated.

A LAMB'S TALE

Walk in with the lamb under your arm. Encourage the children to touch its wool. Let them know that the lamb's name is Woolly .

PART I: (*This part is optional, depending on your storytelling style.*) Read or recite, John 10:11. Ask, "What is a shepherd?" (*Separate the word into "sheep" and "herd" to see if they can better understand the meaning of being taken care of.*) Ask, "Who takes care of us?" (*Parents and other special people.*) Ask, "Who is speaking in the verse I read?" (*Jesus compares himself to a shepherd taking care of us—his sheep.*)

PART II: (*This part is optional.*) One day Jesus talked to his disciple, Peter. He said, "I am the good shepherd, but I want you to be a shepherd too. Feed and take care of my sheep—the big people. Feed and take care of my baby sheep, the little woolly lambs—the boys and girls and babies." And Peter did. (*Encourage them to stroke the lamb.*) Wherever Peter went, he told big people and little people about Jesus, the good shepherd. He shared the good news. "Jesus loves you," he said. Peter took care of the sheep. Peter took care of the little lambs. (*Give time for them to pet the lamb again.*)

PART III (*Telling the story.*) I wonder what it's like to be a woolly lamb. I wonder what it's like to be Woolly. Would you like to know? Here is Woolly's story, a lamb's tale.

My name is Woolly. My mama's name is Bertha. My papa's name is Sam. When I was born my legs were very wobbly. Thin and wobbly. At night I stayed close to mama. She sheltered me from the cold. During the day, I drank her milk. My bones grew strong. Soon I could run and hop and skip and jump. The good shepherd walked in every day. He lifted me up and held me in his arms. He rocked me. I felt cozy.

One day, I smelled something. I sniffed and sniffed. "What's that I my smell?" I asked papa.

"Oh," he said. "The snow is gone. The birds are singing. Flowers are blooming. Spring is here. You smell fresh, green grass."

"What is grass?" I asked.

"It's good to eat," papa said. "It makes you grow."

"Does it taste like mama's milk?" I asked.

"Better." said papa. "You'll see for yourself. The sun is warm today. I'm sure the good shepherd will take us to a place tomorrow, where we can eat and eat until we feel fat and full."

"Yummy," I said and danced around the sheep stall.

The next morning I heard the good shepherd's voice. "Hello, little one," he said. "Are you ready to try the hills?" He carried me out into the bright sunlight and set me down. All the sheep stumbled out of the stall, one after another. There were more little ones. They looked like me. We bounced around and nudged each other. We played tag and Hide and Seek.

"Come, it's time to go," called the shepherd. We trudged along behind. It was hard to stay on the trail. There were so many things to see. We ate and ate. After awhile I didn't like the smell of grass anymore. I looked around. "I wish I could climb a tree," I said. "Or fly through the sky. Or flutter like a moth. Or buzz like a fly." I flapped my ears and shook my head at a butterfly lighting on my nose. What a big, beautiful world!

"Stay here," Mama called. "It's getting late. The good shepherd will soon lead us home."

"I'll be right there," I called and went off to explore the bushes and the trees.

I didn't see the big, slippery rock. Crash, bang. Before I knew it, I was lying at the bottom of a deep, dark hole. Much later, I opened my eyes. How long had I been there? I didn't know. I listened. No sounds. I looked up. The sun was gone. The sky was dark. "Baa," I called. "Baa." I grew weak and tired. It started to rain. My woolly coat was soggy and cold. "Baa," I called feebly.

I lay there a long time. My leg hurt. I couldn't get up. I couldn't walk or skip or jump. "Where is my mama?" I cried. "Where is the good shepherd?"

Then far away I heard the shepherd's voice. "Woolly," he called. "Baa," I said. But he didn't hear me. The voice came closer and closer. "Woolly." Then louder, "Woo-oo-lly!" I took a deep breath and bleated, "Baa."

"There you are," said the shepherd. He slid into the hole. Down. Down. Down. He picked me up. "You little rascal," he said. "How did you get yourself into such a mess?" His voice was kind. He scraped the mud from my legs and back. "I've looked everywhere for you," he said. He held me close. "You poor thing," he muttered.

The good shepherd wrapped me in his coat. "We must hurry, little one," he said. "'I left the other sheep and little lambs alone in the sheep stall." He half ran, half walked, through the dismal rain. It didn't feel dismal to me. "Ah," I murmured. The good shepherd didn't leave me alone in the mud. He left his warm home and came to find me in the cold, wet night. He left the other sheep and carried me home.

I felt warm inside. "The good shepherd loves me. Really loves me." I whispered. Then I closed my eyes and went to sleep.

C. EMPOWERING THE FAMILY

Families Celebrate 50 Days, Easter to Pentecost:

Jesus appeared to the disciples at the Sea of Galilee. After cooking breakfast and eating together, he spent time with them. Jesus had some special words for Peter about feeding and tending the lambs and sheep. One way the faith is passed on and nurture takes place is through story.

This week you may want to:

- Have a family night with no TV. Take time to listen to each other. Share stories and experiences about when you were growing up.

- Take time for stories, told or read, at bedtime.

- Tell a story to a child; your child, a grandchild, or someone else's child.

ASCENSION SUNDAY

YOU SHALL BE MY WITNESSES

Acts 1:15-19

THEME: The church represents Jesus Christ in the world. In today's violent, broken society, it is easier to stand, look up, and engage in a personal piety, than be empowered for sharing the gospel. The good news is only good and joyful if the bearer has experienced and continues to experience it as such. Apart from that, it becomes old news.

A. THE DRAMA OF WORSHIP

Reader's Theater and Speaker: Make this Sunday a Mission Festival. The mission speaker is incorporated into the Reader's Theater and needs to be informed about the process in advance. A choir sings, "Holy Spirit. Come With Power," (EXHIBIT A-1) as an Invocation. The congregation sings, "Praise God and Celebrate the Son!" (EXHIBIT A-5) as a hymn of praise.

The theater group is made up of four youth and adults, who read from center stage. Follow instructions as to the movement of the group. Rehearse in advance. Members make their entries as indicated. If there are no commas or periods at the end of a speaker's line, it is important for the next speaker to break in. Avoid pauses which disrupt the thought sequence. Before you begin rehearsals, plan where the climax of each section and the climax of the reading will be. This helps the readers with voice inflections, crescendos and dimuendos, all part of a dramatic reading. The mission message is presented by 5 as indicated. A choir sings stanzas 1-3, 5-6, of, "It's Jesus Christ, Hallelujah!" (EXHIBIT A-3) as a message response.

B. RESOURCES FOR THE SERVICE OF WORSHIP

Lighting the Pentecost Wreath

A family or extended family comes forward.

Adult/Youth 1:	*Lights candles 1-6. Reads Matthew 11:4-5.*
Older Child 1:	*Reads or recites, John 3:16.*

Older Child 2:	*Reads Matthew 28:19-20.*
Child 1:	*Lights rose candle, #7.*
Child 2:	"Why do we light this seventh candle?"
Adult/Youth 2:	"This candle reminds us of **GOSPEL**. God has given us the good news of Jesus. The good news makes us glad. We want to share this good news with everyone."

The Bulletin Cover

Select a bulletin cover that shows the church representing Jesus Christ in today's world. Or use something like this one.

A Readers' Theater

(*The four readers come in and sit on four stools placed in a row on the stage. They stand in the order 1, 2, 3, 4, positioned from right to left. When ready, readers rise and step forward.*)

1,2,3,4:	(*loudly*) You shall be my witnesses.
1:	You shall receive power when the Holy spirit has come upon you;
2:	and you shall be my witnesses in Jerusalem
3:	and in all Judea
4:	and Samaria
1, 2, 3, 4:	and to the ends of the earth. (*2 moves beside 4. They face each other and 3 and 1 do the same*)
4:	It is so easy to talk about the weather
2:	about friends and daily events,
4:	but so hard to talk about being a Christian; our struggles, our fears, our joys, our sorrows.

3:	It is easy to talk about our jobs, homes, families and hobbies
1:	about school, videos and TV
3:	but hard to know how all this fits in with being a Jesus follower.
1, 2, 3, 4:	(*readers face forward and speak in unison*) But you shall receive power when the Holy spirit has come upon you;
4:	and you shall be my witnesses.
1, 2, 3, 4:	(*unison*) We are, we can and we shall be.....
1:	Empowered,
2:	Great power,
3:	Spirit power,
4:	And witnesses to the One who has redeemed us. (*All readers move around and change positions but keep the same numbers in the reading.*)
2:	Words. Words. 2000 years old words. Do they make sense?
1:	Sometimes I wonder where God is when I'm at school,
4:	Or with the family, or on the job,
2:	Or with friends,
1:	Or on a date,
3:	Or when there's violence on the street—
4:	War, famine and revolution flashes across the screen each night.
1,3:	Sometimes, I wonder and wonder.
5:	(*The speaker rises, stands at pulpit and speaks.*) But you shall receive power when the Holy Spirit has come upon you; and you shall be my witnesses. Your sons and daughters will prophecy, your young men will see visions and your old men will dream dreams. Even on my servants, both men and women, I will pour my Spirit. That's where God is.
1,2,3,4:	(*To congregation*) Did you hear that? That's us. You.
5:	(*urgently*) Why then, do you stand here, looking into the sky?
4:	You shall receive power when the Holy Spirit has come upon you
3:	and you shall be my witnesses.
1:	Amen.
2,3,4:	Amen! (*Hurry down center aisle, turn before they exit and call out from entrance to narthex.*)
1,2,3,4:	(*loudly*) So be it Lord. AMEN. (*5 then delivers message.*)

Families Celebrate 50 Days, Easter to Pentecost:

The good news of Jesus is shared by what we do, what we say and how we live. This week try:

- Have a family talk about ways you could share the good news.

- Say, "I love you," to your parent or child at least once a day.

- Do a kind act for someone who doesn't like you or has hurt your feelings.

- Twice a week, plan a dinner menu, then eat soup.

- Pick up litter and keep God's world beautiful.

- Bring canned good for the needy to a food pantry.

- Invite someone to your home who rarely gets invited by others.

- Set a branch in a pot. Make dove shaped (symbol of God's spirit) sugar cookies and hang on tree. Share these with friends when they come to your house. If they ask, "What does this dove mean?" Say, "The dove reminds us that God is our helper and friend. God loves us."

PENTECOST SUNDAY

A SOUND FROM HEAVEN

Acts 2:1-4

THEME: Jesus' post-Easter appearances to individuals and smaller groups move to a climax at Pentecost. Christ makes his eternal presence known to the gathered community through the Holy Spirit. The intense experience, evidenced by symbols of flames, a violent wind and ecstatic language, introduces a new level of religious encounter that births the church. With the church's nativity, new life, power, courage, and joy break into history. The world is never the same again.

A. THE DRAMA OF WORSHIP

The Easter service began on a low key, climaxing in the recognition scene. Pentecost too, begins on a subdued note, quickly rising to praise and exultation. Present this theme in two parts, one leading into the other.

Scripture as Readers' Theater: The congregation sings, "Holy Spirit, Come With Power," (EXHIBIT A-1) as an Invocation. After the hymn, four readers enter down different aisles of the sanctuary, reciting Acts 2:1 in unison (*or in different languages*). They walk on stage and kneel in prayer, faces turned upwards. Readers speak the Unison Prayer. Following the "Amen," they engage in Scripture as Readers' Theater. This serves as a Call to Worship. (Option: Sing, "Holy Spirit Come With Power," as an Invocation. Follow with The Pentecost Banner Parade [Call to Worship]. Precede the sermon with Scripture as Readers' Theater.)

The Pentecost Banner Parade: Immediately after, the last "Hallelujah" of the Scripture as Readers' Theater, the congregation stands and sings stanzas 1,2,3 and 5,6,7 of, "It's Jesus Christ, Hallelujah!" as a Hymn of Praise. (Hymn option: "Christ the Lord is Risen Today.") The elementary grades sing with the congregation as they parade down the aisles, carrying the Pentecost banners. Four in each group carry the banner, holding it at the corners. When the groups arrive at the front, they separate and several children hang the banners. They return to their places in the pews.

If the option for Scripture as Readers' Theater is used, the parade takes place during the Prelude or after the Invocation hymn.

(This theme provides opportunity for adult baptism, or confirmation, or accepting new members into the church.)

B. RESOURCES FOR THE SERVICE OF WORSHIP

Lighting the Pentecost Wreath

A family or extended family comes forward.

Adult/Youth 1:	*Lights candles 1-7. Reads John 14:16-17a.*
Older Child:	*Reads John 16:13-15.*
Child 1	*Lights the red Pentecost candle, #8.*
Child 2:	"Why do we light this eighth candle?"
Adult/Youth 2:	"This candle reminds us of **POWER**. God's Holy Spirit is with us and gives us the power and courage to be joyful followers of Jesus."

The Bulletin Cover

Replicate the banner design or purchase bulletins that reinforce the theme.

A Unison Prayer

Come Holy Spirit, God of love,
And give us power from above.
Through Jesus Christ, your only son,
Grant us a love that makes us one,
You are the truth, the life, the way.
Help us to share that news today.
Good news, good news, good news , we say.
With joy-filled hearts we kneel and pray,
Come Holy Spirit from above
And fill us with the God of love.

Scripture as Readers' Theater

This dramatic rendering of scripture in a Readers' Theater format, bases the words on Biblical text (NIV). It calls the worshipers to participate in the joy and wonder of Pentecost. The nativity of the church evokes emotions, not unlike those at the nativity of the Christ (Luke 2:14).

(Readers slowly rise as they speak.) (Note the initial process under THE DRAMA OF WORSHIP.)

1,2,3,4:	Suddenly a sound like the blowing of a violent wind came from heaven and filled the whole house where they were sitting.
3:	*(leans forward)* They saw what seemed to be tongues of fire that separated and came to rest on each one of them;
1:	Resting on each one of them,
4:	Resting on each one of them,
2:	Resting on each one of them.

3:	Tongues of fire that separated and came to rest on each one of them.
1, 2, 3, 4:	(*unison*) All of them were filled with the Holy Spirit;
1:	The counselor,
1,2,3,4:	Wonderful Counselor.
4:	The teacher,
1,2,3,4:	Mighty God.
3:	The comforter,
1,2,3,4:	Everlasting Father.
2:	God's power exploding into a new community,
1,2,3,4:	Prince of Peace.
1:	Joy!
3:	Abundant life!
2:	Hope!
4:	Purpose!
1,2,3,4:	A new community of faith. (*As they speak the following, readers move forward to form a circle, leaving an opening at one side.*)
1, 2, 3, 4:	And they began to speak in other tongues as the Spirit enabled them;
4:	Good news to share,
2:	Good news.
1:	(*steps forward*) Then Peter stood up and addressed the crowd;
3:	Courage.
1:	Peter, the denier, stood up and addressed the crowd;
3:	New courage,
1,2,3,4:	Good news to share. (*All move forward*)
3:	Peter received power;
1,2,3,4:	Spirit power.
1, 2, 4:	You will be my witnesses;
4:	Witnesses,
2:	Witnesses,
1:	Witnesses,
1, 2, 3, 4:	(*unison*) You will receive power when the Holy Spirit comes on you, and you will be my witnesses.
3:	Peter said, "Listen to me. What you see and hear is the promised Holy Spirit, poured out by the resurrected Christ, who sits at the right hand of God. (*Readers fall on their knees and stretch out hands, imploring.*)
1, 2, 3, 4:	(*unison - crescendo*) What must we do? What must we do? **What must we do?** (*Quickly get up and form a semi-circle around 3*).

3:	Repent! (*Others chime in with the same word, raising it to a crescendo.*) (*Readers hold out arms, palms facing up, an expression of joy and wonder on their faces.*)
1, 2, 3, 4:	(*amazed*) And about three thousand were added to their number that day; *(the readers move down and exit center aisle. As they walk, they keep repeating the above in the following manner:)*
1:	Were added,
2:	Added,
4:	Added,
3:	On that day there were added
1, 2, 3, 4:	(*unison*) About three thousand souls. *(When they come to the end of the aisle, they turn and call out.)* Hallelujah! Hallelujah!

Closing Hymn for Pentecost Sunday

Sing to the tune of "Lead On, O King Eternal." Alternate melodies are: "The Church's One Foundation," "Sing to the Lord of Harvest," or any other hymn from your hymnal's Metrical Index of Tunes under 7.6.7.6.D. In choosing another tune, make sure the melody and mood of the music fit the words. Double check to make sure all syllables match the music's rhythm.

Lead On, O King of Glory
by Anne Neufeld Rupp

Lead on, O King of Glory and guide us with your might;
Instill in us your courage and put our fears to flight.
Let life be celebration, let want and hunger cease.
Let all our paths be joyous, as we give the world your peace.

Lead on, O King of Glory and open up our soul
To sharing life with others, help us to make them whole.
There's violence in our country, starvation on the street,
Along each land and byway, a suffering Christ we meet.

Lead on, O King of Glory, our Teacher, Master, Lord.
Grant us your deep compassion, enact in us your word.
Wherever you direct us, to share life's bitter night,
We'll start your celebration, and put all fears to flight.

**Families Celebrate 50 Days,
Easter to Pentecost:**

Bake a cake, frost and decorate with many non-extinguishable candles, for a Pentecost Sunday dessert. When family members try to blow out the candles, the flames will keep returning. Use this opportunity to talk about the church, its birth at Pentecost, and the many times attempts have been made to extinguish its light. But without success. Share related stories from your denominational or personal history with your children. Talk about ways your family can be the church in the neighborhood and community where you live. Sing, "Happy birthday, dear church," to the tune of Happy Birthday, using these words:

Happy birthday, dear church. Happy birthday, dear church.

Happy birthday, happy birthday, Happy birthday, dear church.

****

HOLY SPIRIT, COME WITH POWER

Anne N. Rupp   Anne N. Rupp

Moderate tempo

1 Ho-ly Spir-it, come with pow-er, breathe in-to our ach - ing night.
2 Ho-ly Spir-it, come with fi- re, burn us with your pres- ence new.
3 Ho-ly Spir-it, bring your mes-sage, burn and breathe eachword a- new.

We ex-pect you this glad ho-ur, wait-ing for your strength and light.
Let us as one might-y cho-ir sing our hymn of praise to you.
deep in-to our tir- ed liv-ing till we strive your work to do.

We are fear-ful, we are ail-ing, we are weak and self- ish too.
Burn a- way our wast- ed sad-ness, and en- flame us with your word.
Teach us love and trust-ing kind-ness, lend our hands to those who hurt

Break up- on your con- gre- ga-tion, give us vig- or life a- new.
Burst up-on your con- gre- ga-tion, give us glad- ness from a- bove.
Breathe up-on your con- gre- ga-tion and in- spire us with your word,

Lament

Music and words by A. N. Rupp

1. You walked through the crowds with Your gen-tle-ness, Your cour-age and strength touched us
2. You talked with the ones who were fol-low-ing, The par-a-ble les-sons were
3. You ate with Your friends in the eve-ning, You prayed as your time near-er
4. You stood be-fore high priests and rul-ers, You bent as the death hun-ger
5. The world now seems drear-y and emp-ty, The hopes you ful-filled were-n't

too; You held a small child, healed the lame and the blind, And now they have done this to
new; We ea-ger-ly heard your com-passion-filled words, And now they have done this to
drew; "Not my will be done," cried God's on-ly Son, And now they have done this to
grew; A voice, cold and grim, cried, "Cru-ci-fy him!" And now they have done this to
true; Your death on the cross has been ev-'ry-one's loss, Oh, why have they done this to

You.
You.
You. I am a-lone with my sor-row. I am a-lone with my pain.
You.
You.

Lone-li-ness holds me like a child new-ly born, I won't see my Je-sus a-

gain. a - gain (after final chorus) I won't see my Je-sus a-gain.

Used by permission. Copyright © 1978 by Evangel Press, Nappanee, IN 46550. Faith and Life Press, Newton, KS 67114; Mennonite Publishing House, Scottdale, PA 15683. The Foundation Series, Grades 5 and 6. Student Guide Reader, pages 46-47.

IT'S JESUS CHRIST, HALLELUJAH!

Anne N. Rupp   Anne N. Rupp

Lively tempo

1 It's   Je-   sus   Christ,   Hal- le- lu- jah!
2 We've   seen the   Lord,   Hal- le- lu- jah!
3 Let's   share the   news,   Hal- le- lu- jah!
4 A   great sur- prise,   Hal- le- lu- jah!
5 Praise God   for   him,   Hal- le- lu- jah!
6 He'll   give us   power,   Hal- le- lu- jah!
7 Let's   sing for   joy,   Hal- le- lu- jah!

It's   Je-   sus   Christ   Hal- le- lu- jah!
We've   seen the   Lord,   Hal- le- lu- jah!
Let's   share the   news,   Hal- le- lu- jah!
A   great sur- prise,   Hal- le- lu- jah!
Praise God   for   him,   Hal- le- lu- jah!
He'll   give us   power,   Hal- le- lu- jah!
Let's   sing for   joy,   Hal- le- lu- jah!

It's   Je-   sus   Christ,   It's   Je-   sus   Christ,
We've   seen the   Lord,   We've   seen the   Lord,
Let's   share the   news,   Let's   share the   news,
A   great sur- prise,   A   great sur- prise,
Praise God   for   him,   Praise God   for   him,
He'll   give us   power,   He'll   give us   power,
Let's   sing for   joy,   Let's   sing for   joy,

It's   Je-   sus   Christ,   A- men.
We've   seen the   Lord,   A- men.
Let's   share the   news,   A- men.
A   great sur- prise,   A- men.
Praise God   for   him,   A- men.
He'll   give us   power,   A- men.
Let's   sing for   joy,   A- men.   A- men.

I Am Jesus' Little Lamb

WEIL ICH JESU SCHÄFLEIN BIN. 7. 7. 8. 8. 7. 7.

HENRIETTA LUISE VON HAYN, 1778
Tr. WILLIAM F. STEVENSON, 1871

From "Gesangbuch mit Noten"

1. I am Je - sus' lit - tle lamb, Ev - er glad at heart I am;
2. Safe - ly in and out I go, Je - sus loves and keeps me so.
3. Should I not be al - ways glad? None whom Je - sus loves are sad;

Je - sus loves me, Je - sus knows me, All things fair and good He shows me,
When I hun - ger, Je - sus feeds me; When I thirst, my Shep - herd leads me
And when this short life is end - ed, Those whom the Good Shep - herd tend - ed

E - ven calls me by my name; Ev - 'ry day He is the same.
Where the wa - ters soft - ly flow, Where the sweet - est pas - tures grow.
Will be tak - en to the skies, There to dwell in Par - a - dise. A-men.

The Mennonite Hymnary. Mennonite Publication Office, Newton, KS, 1940. #430. Used by permission.

PRAISE GOD AND CELEBRATE THE SON
(A Folk Song)

Anne N. Rupp   Anne N. Rupp

Joyfully

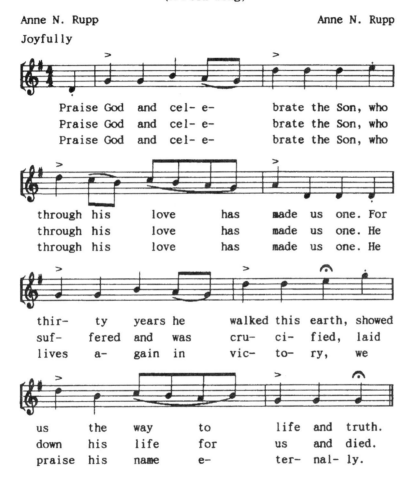

Praise God and cel- e- brate the Son, who
Praise God and cel- e- brate the Son, who
Praise God and cel- e- brate the Son, who

through his love has made us one. For
through his love has made us one. He
through his love has made us one. He

thir- ty years he walked this earth, showed
suf- fered and was cru- ci- fied, laid
lives a- gain in vic- to- ry, we

us the way to life and truth.
down his life for us and died.
praise his name e- ter- nal- ly.

Tune option: "Praise God from whom all blessings flow." (Doxology).

EXHIBIT A-6

During Advent, the lighting of the candles on the Advent wreath is an important part of many worship services in both church and home. During Lent, some may feature a Lenten triad during the weeks before Easter. Rarely do we find an emphasis such as this, during the weeks when we walk towards Pentecost. Yet, Pentecost brings to us the advent of the Holy Spirit, in ways unknown to most of God's people earlier. It is a fulfillment of the Joel 2:28-29 prophecy. Pentecost brings the birth of the church. We do well to find ways to anticipate that time which rests between the two great Jewish feasts of Passover and Pentecost. One way to remind us that these 50 days are important is by weekly candle lighting services. Another way is to read and reflect on the post-resurrection stories in the gospels and the post-Pentecost events in the book of Acts. The following directions give instructions for creating a wreath or triad. They identify candle colors to be used, beginning with a triad of three white candles to represent the Trinity. These are followed by two pink and two rose candles. This represents movement towards the red Pentecost candle. Size of wreath and candles is not given but may be adapted to each particular situation.

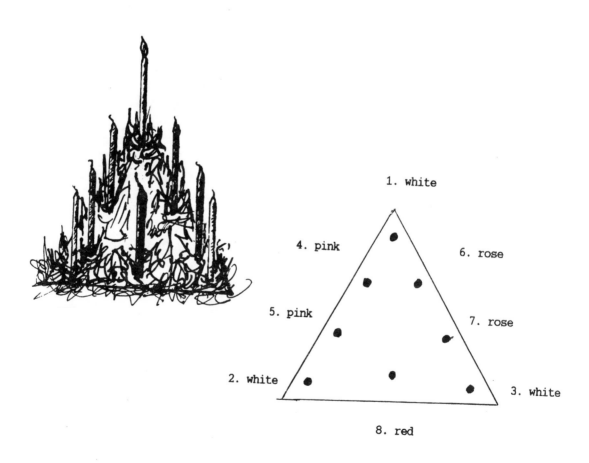

1. white
4. pink
6. rose
5. pink
7. rose
2. white
3. white
8. red

Part II

CHILDREN WORSHIP AND LEARN

Introduction

For most children, the important days of the church year are Christmas and Easter. During December they wait eagerly throughout Advent for the long-awaited Christmas Day. They light Advent candles, make and send cards, sing carols, view Christmas programs and much more. The emphasis is on moving from darkness to light as the anticipation grows. Because Christmas is the climax of this 'waiting' time, children are able to relate the birth of Christ to the season of Advent quite well.

In midwinter and into spring, the children make another journey—from Lent towards Easter. Lent sets a different mood. It is more reflective, fewer activities are planned in both church and home, and looking forward to Easter comes only a short time before the event itself. It may be more difficult for children to relate Lent to Easter, than Advent to Christmas. Even adults may think of Lent as moving towards Good Friday—the crucifixion. But children recognize that Lent is an important time in the church. They know that after a few hours of weekend mourning, Easter joy will burst upon them. Easter is not as commercialized as Christmas nor is it usually a family or gift-giving time, so anticipation is brief and less pronounced. But children do look forward to this special, celebrative time of year.

But what happens during the 50 days from Easter to Pentecost? Should this not be another time of waiting? These seven weeks are filled with a series of events that lead towards the climax of Divine purpose for God's people, the founding of the church. Yes, Christ was birthed among us, Christ arose and ascended, but without Pentecost there would be no church today.

Incarnation and Resurrection are theological concepts beyond a child's reasoning power. A child doesn't understand the significance of Christmas and Easter as an adult does. That's why we translate these God-occasions into language and meanings the child can understand (depending on age and stage of development). Pentecost also requires that comprehensible language, concept, and experience be brought into the child's world. The suggestions for worship and teaching in, Walking Towards Pentecost, Part II, attempt to do just that. The post-resurrection experiences and Pentecost are presented in a language the children can understand.

The following suggestions require one hour of Church School time on Sunday mornings, from Easter to Pentecost. The goal is to put the post Easter events into a sequence that leads up to Pentecost, 50 days after Easter. Children will begin to recognize the importance of Pentecost as they experience and participate in the movement towards it. Consequently, they will experience the joy and excitement of those stories and relate the themes to their own lives. They will also gain a better understanding of the young churches in Acts and the church today.

PLANNING AHEAD

Several weeks before Easter, teachers meet and plan for the series to come. Each Sunday consists of two parts:

A. ASSEMBLY — 15-20 minutes.

During this time together, teachers act out the story for children, from pre-school through Junior age (an effective teaching tool). At your meetings, study the objectives set for the lessons, engage in thorough Bible study suggested for the eight Sundays and outline scripts which will make it possible for teachers to act and ad lib the scenes. Use the guidelines suggested for each Sunday as a basis for your brief skits. After this is done, assign parts. (For the sake of continuity and young children's comprehension, it is advisable for the one who assumes the role of Jesus on Easter morning, to maintain that role throughout.)

Costuming is optional. If you use it, keep it simple. Bathrobes are fine, but you can make simple robes by sewing together 45" strips of cotton, leaving room for armholes on either side. Cut out a neck and tie a cord around the waist. Sandals or barefoot are optional. Use your imagination (I have used a ball of yarn taped to my chin, and tied behind my ears, for a beard). If you don't use costume, use some identifying label such as a headband with a name on it, or a giant name tag hung from the neck.

The skit is only one part of the Assembly. The children learn a theme song, "It's Jesus Christ, Hallelujah" and add stanzas from week to week. Additional songs, prayers, responses and direct participation, are all part of a plan to help the worshipers become involved in the experience. Study the process of each session carefully.

B. CLASSROOM— 40-45 minutes.

After the Assembly, children move to their classrooms as indicated. Through parades, singing and other active participation, the walk to their rooms links Assembly to Classroom, and provides the continuity and transition needed. Children meet in three groups, Pre-School to Kindergarten, Primary and Junior.

Before studying the sessions, teachers need to make a huge floor map on newsprint. The map covers one side of the classroom. For Juniors, outline Palestine on the map. For the younger ages, outline only Judea, so that their 'walks' are longer. Teachers tape down paper footsteps leading towards and into the classrooms. These footsteps continue each week, providing a walking tour to the place where the day's event takes place. (You may want to help younger children outline their feet in advance and use these patterns for footprints.) For example, the first story takes place in JERUSALEM, so that's where the footsteps stop. Footsteps are added or changed each Sunday after that, depending on the story. This helps the children see the movements of the risen Christ as he reveals himself to more than 500 (1 Corinthians 15:5-6) during the pre-Pentecost weeks. Juniors don't use the footstep approach, but rather learn to identify a number of places where Jesus' earlier ministry took place. Study the instructions at the beginning of the Classroom session to get a better understanding of how this process works for your age group.

The three classroom sessions are age appropriate. Each builds on the theme and the earlier worship experience. At the beginning of each session a list of materials needed is followed by preparation steps. Attempts have been made to keep all materials as simple as possible, but you will need to spend time in advance, gathering or making your materials, and studying the lesson process. Each session involves movement, participation and steps towards helping the children understand and re-live the original experience. The Primary (Seventh Sunday) and Junior (Sixth Sunday) classes will also participate in actual experience through ministry to others. (This may require more of a teacher's time but is well worth the energy expended.)

On the last Sunday, Pentecost, the children will not go to their classrooms. After the Assembly, they will stay in the fellowship hall (or another designated area) and enjoy a Birth of the Church party. Games and activities are listed. If your Church School is large, you may either need to add more activities, or departmentalize, and have two parties going at the same time.

WHAT A HAPPY DAY!

John 20:11-18

OBJECTIVE: To feel the joy and excitement of the resurrection.

GETTING READY: Prepare and do the following in advance:

❑ Assign teachers to the roles of Mary and Jesus. Mary must be able to sing solo.

❑ Mary learns the songs listed below and also, "It's Jesus Christ, Hallelujah!"

❑ Ask someone to read the passage while Mary and Jesus pantomime the story or have them act it out, using their own words.

❑ Create a garden scene using a few potted flowers or plants.

❑ Make a sign, JERUSALEM, and stand on an easel at the front of the room.

❑ Teachers, according to grades are given the suggestions for planning their class time, listed below.

A. ASSEMBLY

1. Individual teachers sit near the aisle, next to their children.

2. Mary walks in singing the children's hymn, "For God So Loved Us" Hymnal: A Worship Book. Elgin, IL: Brethren Press; Newton, KS: Faith and Life Press; Scottdale, PA: Mennonite Publishing House, 1992, #167. She motions the children to join her in the chorus of each stanza.

Mary stops near a plant and stands, shoulders drooping, head down as though crying. Jesus enters quietly from the side. Mary and Jesus act out the scene from John 20:11-18 where she recognizes him.

Mary falls on her knees and reaches up to him, hands clasped. In this position she sings the chorus of "How Great Thou Art," The United Methodist Hymnal. Nashville, TN: Abingdon Press, 1989, #77.

Jesus tells Mary to go and share the good news with his followers. As Jesus quietly exits, Mary faces the children and joyfully sings stanza 1 of the theme song, "It's Jesus Christ, Hallelujah!" (EXHIBIT A-3) twice. She motions teachers and children to sing with her the second time. Mary hurries down the aisle and calls out to the children, "Jesus is alive! Jesus is alive! Come, let's go tell everybody!" (*Jesus quietly exits.*)

Mary urges the teachers and children to follow her down the hallway towards their classrooms and to call out, "Jesus is alive! Jesus is alive!" Teachers move into the aisle, urgently beckon their children and rush out. Encourage spontaneity, shouting and enthusiasm.

B. CLASSROOM

PRE-SCHOOL TO KINDERGARTEN

Materials needed:

❑ floor map with footsteps leading to Jerusalem.

❑ age appropriate picture book with the story of the resurrection.

❑ crayons or colored markers

❑ picture or cut-out of Jesus

❑ a large smile face for the teacher and smaller faces for the children.

❑ thin 12" inch dowels, one for each child.

❑ a hand mirror

❑ cupcakes, frosting, birthday candles and pastel decors or candy.

❑ punch or orange juice.

Preparation:

❑ Make the floor map, following the instructions in the Introduction. Mark in JERUSALEM.

❑ From yellow construction paper or posterboard, cut round circles for smile faces. On the teacher's, draw a sad face on one side and a happy face on the other. On the children's draw happy faces on both sides. Cut two slits in the children's smile faces at top and bottom and insert a thin 12" dowel. Tape in place.

❑ Make and frost colorful cupcakes. Top with candles.

❑ Prepare the juice or punch.

Time with the children:

• Teacher moves ahead of the children. Welcome them as they arrive. Walk on the map with them, following the footsteps to JERUSALEM. Children this age can't conceptualize a map but they will enjoy the little walk. Pretend it's like a stroll in the park today. Draw attention to things or people you see along the road. Continue this approach each Sunday.

• Sit in a circle. Ask, "Are you ever sad? How does your face look when you are sad?" Talk. Then say, "Jesus' friends were very sad." Show the sad face. Make a few comments and move into the story using the picture book. At the end say, "Now they were happy." Show the smile face.

• "Where is Jesus?" game. Hide the figure of Jesus and ask the children to look for Jesus. When they have found the figure, return to the circle and say, "Jesus' friends went to the tomb. It was empty. They couldn't find Jesus. His friend Mary, cried and cried. Then she heard a voice. It said, "Mary!" It was Jesus. She had found Jesus. Mary was glad." Hope up the smile face again.

- Note that Easter is a happy, happy time. Give them each a smile circle and ask them to draw a happy face on it. Parade around the room, shouting, "Happy Easter! Happy Easter!"

- Help the children frost and decorate the cupcakes. Give them candles to put in the center of each one.

- Arrange the cupcakes on the table. Light the candles. Ask them to hold up the smile faces again. Ask if they can turn their faces into smile faces. Let them look in the mirror.

- Again repeat, "Easter is a happy day. Jesus is alive. We can talk to him. Jesus is our friend. Sing the following song several times (to the tune of Happy Birthday).

    Happy Easter to you, Happy Easter to you,
    Happy Easter, dear Jesus, Happy Easter to you.

- Eat together and close class time with a simple sentence prayer.

PRIMARY

Materials needed:

❑ floor map with footsteps leading to Jerusalem.

❑ stiff paper for stick figures and a square of felt.

❑ a flannelboard.

❑ pattern for baby chicks and fluorescent yellow markers.

❑ hardboiled, colored eggs for all children.

❑ crackers, salt and pepper.

❑ punch or orange juice.

Preparation:

❑ Make the floor map, following the instructions in the Introduction. Mark in JERUSALEM.

❑ Prepare the resurrection story and practice several times.

❑ Draw and cut stick figures in different sizes and shapes. Draw different facial expressions on them. Back with felt.

❑ Cut out several chick patterns and purchase yellow markers.

❑ Boil and color the eggs. Arrange them on green confetti or shredded tissue.

❑ Buy crackers.

❑ Prepare the juice or punch.

Time with the children:

- Teacher moves ahead of the children. As they arrive, ask them to walk on the map, following the footsteps to JERUSALEM. Children this age may not grasp the full meaning of a map. Put it into today's context by making statements such as, "This is the land where Jesus lived. This is the road where he walked. Today the walk is about as far as from here to _____ (*designate a familiar landmark*). Continue this approach each Sunday.

- Sit in a circle and place the flannelboard near you. Ask, "Are you ever in an unhappy mood?" Share. Then say, "Jesus' followers were very unhappy." As you move through the story of the resurrection, select and adhere different stick figures to the board, demonstrating different moods of the day.

- Say, "Easter is a happy day. Jesus died and came back to life. Jesus is alive. That makes us happy at Easter." Talk about the many symbols we use at Easter to remind us of new life—flowers, green grass, baby bunnies, baby chicks and more.

- Have children each cut out and color one or more baby chicks. They may take these home or decorate the room with them.

- Note that another new life symbol at Easter is the egg. Move to the table and follow this Greek custom: Children take an egg and face each other in twos. They crack their eggs against each other and the first child says, "Christ is risen!" The second one responds with, "Christ is risen indeed!" The next two follow until everyone around the table has done this.

- Eat the eggs and crackers.

- Sing the following song (to the tune of Happy Birthday).

  Happy Easter to you, Happy Easter to you,
  Happy Easter, dear Jesus, Happy Easter to you.

JUNIOR

Materials needed:

- ❑ floor map and markers.
- ❑ map of Palestine and New Testaments.
- ❑ several sheets of paper, each a different, bright color.
- ❑ butterfly pattern, colored tissue paper and wire coat hangers.
- ❑ stiff paper, thread and colored markers.
- ❑ raisin bread
- ❑ punch or orange juice.
- ❑ copies of *The Response of Praise*.

Preparation:

❑ Make the floor map, following the instructions in the Introduction.

❑ Lay out markers and other map materials. Select seven main areas of Jesus' earlier ministry in Galilee (Samaria or Judea). Write a number for each one beginning with #1 at the earliest point of ministry.

❑ Once identified and discussed, students draw a road from Jerusalem back to #7, #6, #5 and so on, one each Sunday.

❑ Study the resurrection story according to John 20:11-18 and also 1 Corinthians 15:12-21.

❑ Draw and cut out several large butterfly patterns.

❑ Buy, frost and decorate a loaf of raisin bread or make a sweet Easter bread.

❑ Prepare the juice or punch.

❑ Make copies of the *Response of Praise* (see next page).

Time with the students:

• Teacher arrives ahead of the class members. Direct them to the map and ask them where the resurrection occurred. Students mark JERUSALEM on the map. Ask a question like, "Where did Jesus come from before he arrived in Jerusalem? Direct them to #7 on the map. Help them identify the name of the place and what occurred there during Jesus' ministry. Students mark the place on the map and connect it to Jerusalem with the road.

• Students move to their places. Ask them to define the word, "mood." Discuss different moods they have at different times. What causes these moods?

• Divide the class into teams of two and ask each team to study the John 20 story, writing down all the moods they find in this story. Discuss.

• Note that today is Easter, a time of celebration, joy and excitement. Why is the resurrection exciting? What does it matter to us?

• Ask students to read 1 Corinthians 15:12-21. Paul points out that the resurrection is the essence of the good news. Jesus' resurrection not only means that his presence is with us at all times, it also promises that after death we too shall be resurrected to new life with God. The followers of Jesus always live in hope.

• The butterfly, going through metamorphosis, from cocoon to winged creature is a symbol of new life. Students cut out butterflies from stiff paper using this pattern or designing their own. They cut about 1/3 inch within the wings and back with colored tissue. Fasten with varying lengths of thread to the coat hanger to make a mobile.

• Gather around the table and draw attention to the bread. Note that in Russia, a special sweet bread called Pascha (which means Passover or Easter) is baked, decorated and eaten. It is a reminder that Jesus is the Bread of Life. Cut slices and after they have eaten, pass out and read the response.

Response of Praise

Leader:	Jesus said, "I am the bread of Life." He came many years ago to show us what this means.
Class:	Happy, happy Easter.
Leader:	Jesus said, "I am the bread of life." He gave his life for us, he rose that we may live again.
Class:	Happy, happy Easter.
Leader:	No one can live without bread or food, No one can live without Jesus; he gives us real life.
All:	Happy, happy Easter! Jesus is our bread of life. Hallelujah!

COME OVER TO MY HOUSE

Luke 24: 13-29

OBJECTIVE: To experience Jesus as an ever present friend.

GETTING READY: Prepare and do the following in advance:

    ❑ Check to make sure the teacher taking on the Jesus role is available.

    ❑ Assign teachers to the roles of Cleopas and friend.

    ❑ Make a sign, EMMAUS, and stand on an easel at the front of the room.

    ❑ Write the words of the unison prayer, "STAY WITH US," on a chalkboard.

    ❑ Teachers, according to grades are given suggestions for planning their class time, listed below.

A. ASSEMBLY

1. Individual teachers sit near the aisle, next to their children.

2. Cleopas and friend walk slowly down the aisle as they act out the Luke 24 scene. They talk about how they hoped Jesus would become their leader. Now they are sad because he died. They don't know how they will get along without their friend. Jesus quietly follows them. After awhile he asks to join their conversation. They don't recognize him but as they talk, they soon develop a warm, understanding relationship. They listen closely as Jesus speaks and respond with words such as, "You're a real friend. You understand how sad and lonely we are." When they reach the EMMAUS sign, the two eagerly invite Jesus to come to their home. Jesus agrees and takes the sign EMMAUS.

Cleopas' friend asks the children to bow their heads and the two lead the group in the following unison prayer:

> *STAY WITH US*
> Stay with us Lord Jesus, we need you every day.
> Be our friend and comforter, guide us on our way. Amen.

3. Cleopas asks the children to join in the singing of "Jesus Loves Me" <u>Hymnal: A Worship Book.</u> Elgin, IL: Brethren Press; Newton, KS: Faith and Life Press; Scottdale, PA: Mennonite Publishing House, 1992, #341.

4. Jesus steps forward and says, "I am Jesus. I am always with you—in your classroom, at school, in your home. Wherever you go, I am with you. I'm your friend." Jesus picks up the EMMAUS sign and asks the children to follow him to their classrooms. All sing stanza 1, "It's Jesus Christ, Hallelujah!" (EXHIBIT A-3) as they go. Jesus escorts the children to their rooms and wishes each group a happy day. Cleopas and friend bring up the rear.

B. CLASSROOM

Pre-school To Kindergarten

Materials needed:

- ☐ floor map with footsteps leading to EMMAUS.
- ☐ pictures from magazines featuring friends.
- ☐ teacher's smile face (*see last Sunday*).
- ☐ paper and crayons.
- ☐ newsprint or shelf paper.
- ☐ several balls of heavy yarn.

Preparation:

- ☐ Mark EMMAUS on the map and extend the footsteps (Luke 24:13).
- ☐ Cut pictures of friends from magazines.
- ☐ Fold a long, narrow paper numerous times and fit the enlarged pattern on it. The hands of the figure touch the folds. Cut around the figure but leave hands intact. When you open the chain, the figures will form a chain. If more chains are needed, cut as below and tape to the first chain.

- ☐ Make warm fuzzies for each child. Wind yarn around a glass many times, slip off, tie in the middle, cut ends and ruffle into a ball.

Time With the Children:

- Teacher enters and welcomes each child. Walk on the map with them, first to JERUSALEM and from there to EMMAUS.

- Sit in a circle and talk about the friend pictures you show them. Ask, "Who is your best friend?" "What do you like to do with your friend?" "Is Jesus your friend?"

- Tell this short story. Make sound effects as you go, such as the tramping of feet, birds singing, etc. Children imitate the sounds and actions.

One day, two of Jesus' friends were <u>walking</u> on the road. They were going home. The sky was blue. Birds <u>sang</u> in the trees. Wind <u>whispered</u> in the branches. It was a happy day. But Jesus' friends were not happy. Jesus' friends felt <u>sad</u>. (*Show sad face*). They talked about their friend Jesus. "I miss him so much!" said Cleopas. <u>Tears</u> rolled down his cheeks. Cleopas and his friend didn't know Jesus was alive. They <u>walked</u> and <u>walked</u>. Slowly. <u>Tromp</u>. <u>Tromp</u>. <u>Tromp</u>.

"Don't be sad," said a voice behind them. The voice made them <u>smile</u>. (*Show smile face*). They didn't know it was Jesus. "Come to our house," they said. "Come and be our friend!"

"Yes, I'll come," said Jesus. And he did.

- Give paper and crayons to the children and let them draw their version of this story. When done, ask each one, "Would you like to tell us about your picture?" Share.

- Say, "Friends belong together." Open the human paper chain and pass around until it forms a complete class circle. Suggest they bow their heads and all say, "Thank you Jesus for friends."

- Say, "Friends make us feel warm and loving. We like to have them come to our house." Pass out the warm fuzzies. Let them press the soft balls to their faces and play with them.

- Say, "Jesus is our friend. He loves us and is always with us." Sing the following song several times (*to the tune of Happy Birthday*).

  Jesus is my best friend, Jesus is my best friend.
  Thank you God for dear Jesus. Jesus is my best friend.

PRIMARY

Materials needed:

- ☐ floor map with footsteps leading to EMMAUS.
- ☐ brown paper lunch bags and markers.
- ☐ colored sheets of paper and crayons.

Preparation:

- ☐ Mark EMMAUS on the map and extend the footsteps (Luke 24:13).
- ☐ Make one paper bag puppet using markers to draw in the face.

Time with the children:

- As the children arrive, ask them to walk on the map, first to JERUSALEM and from there to EMMAUS. (*See First Sunday guidelines.*)

- Move to the table. Briefly review the story acted out in assembly. Ask questions such as, "Why were Jesus' friends sad?" Divide the class into groups of three and give each group three brown bags. They make puppets of Cleopas, friend and Jesus. The groups take turns acting out the story, using their own words.

- Play a short game based on, "My grandmother went to France and took...." and call this, "If Jesus came to my house for supper we would eat...." Each child adds to that which has been said by the previous ones. If one misses, he/she drops out and the game continues until only one is left.

- Say, "Jesus loves us and is always with us. He is our friend." Sing the following song (*to the tune of Happy Birthday*). The children may want to make up other words or add stanzas.

    Jesus is my best friend, Jesus is my best friend.
    Thank you God for dear Jesus. Jesus is my best friend.

    Be near me today. Be near me today.
    Be near me, Lord Jesus. Be near me today.

JUNIOR

Materials needed:

☐ floor map and markers.

☐ map of Palestine and New Testaments.

☐ shoe box, small sheets of paper and pencils.

☐ tape recorder and cassette tape.

Preparation:

☐ Lay out markers and other map materials.

☐ Open a New Testament at Luke 24:13.

☐ Study the story according to Luke 24:13-29. Reflect on the themes of hope, disappointment, sadness and comfort.

☐ Cut a slot in the top of a shoe box.

☐ Write the names of students on individual sheets of paper.

☐ ADVANCE PLANNING: Invite a present or former missionary or service worker to speak to your class on Ascension Sunday (*seventh Sunday*). Reserve for specific time and place.

Time with the students:

- As students arrive, move to the map. Ask them where today's story took place. Suggest someone read Luke 24:13. Others check a map to find out the direction of EMMAUS from Jerusalem. Students mark EMMAUS on the map and connect it to Jerusalem. Review #7. Ask, "Where did Jesus come from before _____" Direct them to #6 on the map. Help them identify the name of the place and what occurred there during Jesus' ministry. Students mark the place on the map and connect it to #7 with the road.

- Divide students into groups of three. Each group studies Luke 24:13-29. Ask each group to list all the questions they have about this story. (*Questions that may come up are, "How come they didn't recognize Jesus?" "Why didn't Jesus tell them who he was?"*) When finished, discuss the questions. If they can't come up with satisfactory responses, ask for volunteers to interview adults in the church after class and record their responses. Suggest they start with, "May we ask you some questions?"

- Inform them that several 'sightings' of the resurrected Christ took place at the tomb on Easter morning. Now, we have another one that takes place later that day, several miles from Jerusalem. 1 Corinthians 15:6 says there were more than 500 sightings but only a few are recorded. Note that today's story is unfinished. Give each student the sheet of paper with his/her name on it. Suggest they pretend to be Cleopas or friend. Now write a first person account about how the story might end. Will Jesus stay overnight? Will we find out who this mysterious stranger is? When finished, students fold their sheets and put into the shoe box. Note that the responses will be read next Sunday.

- Draw attention to the many feelings in this story. Note these feelings are not unlike those we experience in our lives. Ask them to respond to the following:

  When I hope for something I _____.

  When I'm disappointed I _____.

  When I'm sad and lonely, I _____.

  When I lose a friend I _____.

  When I make a new friend I _____.

  When friends come to my house I _____.

- Sing, "What a Friend We Have in Jesus," Hymns of Glorious Praise. Springfield, MO: Gospel Publishing House, 1969, #403, or close with sentence prayers.

HELLO, JESUS!

Luke 24:30-33a

OBJECTIVE: To recognize Jesus in everyday events.

GETTING READY: Prepare and do the following in advance:

❑ Check to make sure the teacher taking on the Jesus role is available.

❑ Check with teachers who took on Cleopas and friend role last Sunday to make sure they're available.

❑ Place a small table and three chairs on one side with a loaf of unsliced bread on it.

❑ Put the sign, EMMAUS on an easel, behind the table.

❑ Teachers, according to grades are given suggestions for planning their class time, listed below.

A. ASSEMBLY

1. Individual teachers sit near the aisle, next to their children.

2. Cleopas, friend and Jesus enter from the side. Cleopas welcomes Jesus. They sit down. Friend asks Jesus to say table grace. Jesus invites the children to say grace with him in unison, using the following words:

   "Come Lord Jesus, be our guest and let this food to us be blessed."

3. Jesus breaks the bread and hands a piece to the two followers. They look at each other and whisper, "It's him!" The whispers get louder and louder, until they finally shout, "It's him! Jesus!" They talk excitedly to each other and as they do so, Jesus gets up quietly and walks out.

4. The followers wonder where he went. They're sure he'll be back. They get up and tell the children how they felt when this stranger came up to them on the walk to Emmaus. Now they know that it was Jesus. They tell the children the good news that Jesus is everywhere. They'll never feel alone again. All sing stanzas 1-2, "It's Jesus Christ, Hallelujah! (EXHIBIT A-3).

5. Cleopas and friend, break the bread into small pieces and give them to the children to eat. They tell the children to remember when they eat, that Jesus is with us wherever we go. They turn this into a chant and all children speak with them in unison about three or four times, "JESUS IS WITH US WHEREVER WE GO."

6. When finished the two look at each other and excitedly say, "We've told the good news to these children. It's very, very late but we've got to go to Jerusalem and tell the disciples!"

They invite the children to go with them and to sing stanza 3, "It's Jesus Christ, Hallelujah!" (EXHIBIT A-3) as they walk along the hallways. Teachers and students follow. As Cleopas and friend reach the doorways of individual classrooms, they stop at the door and say to that class, "Go to Jerusalem. Tell the good news. Jesus is everywhere."

B. CLASSROOM

Pre-school To Kindergarten

Materials needed:

- ❑ floor map with footsteps leading from Emmaus to Jerusalem.
- ❑ a large cardboard box and markers.
- ❑ teacher's smile face (see *First Sunday*)
- ❑ a gift wrapped box and Love Cookies.

Preparation:

- ❑ Place return footsteps, EMMAUS to JERUSALEM on the map.
- ❑ Prepare and learn the simple story song.
- ❑ Make or buy sugar cookies. Use a frosting tip to write the word LOVE on each cookie.
- ❑ Place the cookies in a box and gift wrap.

Time with the children:

- Teacher arrives ahead of the children. Welcome them as they come in. Walk on the map with them, first to JERUSALEM, then to EMMAUS and back to JERUSALEM.

- Sit in a circle, hold hands and sing, "Jesus Loves Me" Hymnal: A Worship Book, Elgin, IL: Brethren Press; Newton, KS: Faith and Life Press; Scottdale, PA: Mennonite Publishing House, 1992, #341.

- Stand the cardboard box on end and illustrate the story by drawing stick figures on it go. Tell this story:

  Do you like surprises? Lisa liked surprises. Big surprises. Little surprises. One day Lisa said to Daddy, "I miss grandma and grandpa."

  Daddy said, "They are far, far away. Would you like to talk to grandma on the phone?"

  "O, yes," said Lisa. Daddy dialed. Lisa listened. The phone rang. No answer. The phone rang and rang. Still no answer.

  "Nobody there," Lisa said and hung up. Then she heard a noise outside. It sounded like a car honking. She ran to the door and opened it. It was grandpa and grandma.

  "Surprise," grandpa called. Grandma and grandpa hugged her real close.

- The children will want to talk about the special, loving people in their lives. Then move on to say, "Here's another surprise story." Sing or recite the following, using the indicated actions. Encourage them to do the actions with you. (*Remember that children will respond better to singing than talking.*) At the end, shout, "Surprise!" Call out several times and ask the children to shout with you.

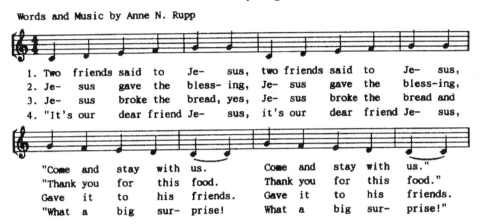

TWO FRIENDS AND JESUS
A Story Song

Words and Music by Anne N. Rupp

1. Two friends said to Je- sus, two friends said to Je- sus,
2. Je- sus gave the bless- ing, Je- sus gave the bless- ing,
3. Je- sus broke the bread, yes, Je- sus broke the bread and
4. "It's our dear friend Je- sus, it's our dear friend Je- sus,

"Come and stay with us. Come and stay with us."
"Thank you for this food. Thank you for this food."
Gave it to his friends. Gave it to his friends.
"What a big sur- prise! What a big sur- prise!"

- Join in a Happy March around the room, clapping and marching as all call out, "Happy! Happy! What a big surprise!"

- Point to the gift wrapped surprise box. All gather around the table. Unwrap the box, open and take out the LOVE cookies. Tell them the words spells "Love." Say, "These surprise LOVE cookies remind us that Jesus is with us." Eat the cookies.

- Remember Jesus is with us: when we play, when we laugh, when Mommy or Daddy hugs us, when we have fun, in this room, at home, at school or any other place.

- Sing the following song several times (to the tune of Happy Birthday).

  We're glad you are here. We're glad you are here.
  We're glad you're here, Jesus. We're glad you are here.

PRIMARY

Materials needed:

❑ floor map with footsteps leading from Emmaus to Jerusalem.

❑ family magazines featuring pictures of relationships.

❑ one sheet posterboard.

❑ scissors and glue.

Preparation:

- ❏ Place return footsteps, EMMAUS to JERUSALEM on the map.

- ❏ Prepare and learn the simple story song.

- ❏ Place the posterboard on the table and lay the magazines and scissors nearby.

Time with the children:

- Teacher arrives ahead of the children. As they come in, ask them to walk on the map, from EMMAUS back to JERUSALEM.

- Sit in a circle. Sing or recite "Two Friends and Jesus" using the indicated actions. Ask them to do the actions with you. After singing it several times the children may want to take on roles in the story and pantomime the scenes as you sing them. (For a more simple version, see the previous page.) At the end, shout, "Surprise!" Call out several times and ask the children to shout with you.

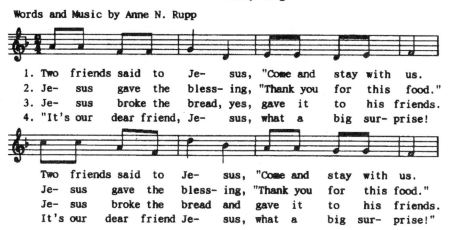

TWO FRIENDS AND JESUS
A Story Song

Words and Music by Anne N. Rupp

1. Two friends said to Je- sus, "Come and stay with us.
2. Je- sus gave the bless- ing, "Thank you for this food."
3. Je- sus broke the bread, yes, gave it to his friends.
4. "It's our dear friend, Je- sus, what a big sur- prise!

Two friends said to Je- sus, "Come and stay with us.
Je- sus gave the bless- ing, "Thank you for this food."
Je- sus broke the bread and gave it to his friends.
It's our dear friend Je- sus, what a big sur- prise!"

- Ask, "What was the big, happy surprise in this story? *(1. Jesus was alive—their friend was back. 2. Jesus was eating with them right in their own home.)* Sometimes we need to be reminded that our friend Jesus is everywhere—in ordinary places like:

  ★when a favorite person hugs or holds us

  ★when we walk in the park

  ★when we play outdoors

  ★at mealtime

  ★at bedtime

  ★in school, church or a family car (ask them to volunteer others).

- Give them magazines and scissors to cut out pictures to show where Jesus is with us. Glue onto the poster board to create a collage. Stand around the collage and say, "Please tell us about your pictures." Note how working together gives us many ideas of where Jesus is with us.

- Sing the following song (to the tune of Happy Birthday).

> *We're glad you are here. We're glad you are here.*
> *We're glad you're here, Je-sus. We're glad you are here.*
>
> *We're glad you're at home. We're glad you're at home.*
> *We're glad you're here, Je-sus. We're glad you're at home.*
>
> *We're glad you're at school. We're glad you're at school.*
> *We're glad you're here Je-sus. We're glad you're at school.*

(The children may want to add other stanzas.)

JUNIOR

Materials needed:

❑ map of Palestine and New Testaments.

❑ shoe box with story endings from last Sunday.

❑ an adult dressed as policeman or carrying a badge.

Preparation:

❑ Lay out markers and other map materials.

❑ Study the story according to Luke 24:28-35.

❑ Contact and plan with an adult who takes on the officer role.

Time with the students:

- As students arrive, move towards the map. Ask them where today's story took place. Where did it begin and where does it end? Note that the two are retracing their steps—from Emmaus back to Jerusalem. Students connect a return route to Jerusalem. Review #7 and 6. Ask, "Where did Jesus come from before #6?" Direct them to #5 on the map. Help them identify the name of the place and what occurred there during Jesus' ministry. Students mark the place on the map and connect it to #6 with the road.

- Note that today's story is a continuation of last week. Ask, "Did the story end differently than you expected?" Students pull responses from the shoe box and read them aloud. They compare the endings to those of today's skits. How were they different? Same? Ask, "At what point did the two recognize Jesus?" "What did the simple act of breaking bread remind them of?" (*Discuss—times they ate together or the feeding of the five thousand or the Last Supper.*) "If you had been there, how do you think you would have responded?"

- Note that all four gospels tell the stories of the resurrection. They are not told in the same way, but each one emphasizes that the stone was rolled away, that God's mighty power was at work, and that both men and women had seen him on resurrection morning. Now the gospels tell stories about 'sightings' after the resurrection. Different gospels tell different stories. Why are they in the New Testament?

- At this point, the officer bursts in waving a search warrant. He/she confiscates all the Bibles and tells them they're all under house arrest for having an illegal meeting. The officer says severely, "Don't even think of trying to escape. Guards are posted outside the door." Officer leaves.

- Students may be bewildered. Tell them this was the situation of the early church. The gospels were written many years after Christ's resurrection. The church was being persecuted and the writer's included these post resurrection stories of followers who had seen Jesus in the most ordinary places and at the most ordinary times. (*The gospels only tell a few stories. There were many more. Ask them to look up 1 Corinthians 15:4-8.*) Stories of these 'sightings' were included in the gospels to help the young Christians believe in a resurrected Christ. Believing in his power and presence gave them courage during times of imprisonment and torture.

- What difference does it make, if we think of Jesus as being with us everywhere? Someone wrote a book about practicing the presence of Jesus—thinking of Jesus' hand on our arm or shoulder at whatever we do and wherever we are. Think about that!

    ★Jesus is in our homes, at school, and wherever we go.

    ★Jesus comes to us in our relationships, through other people, ordinary situations or experiences and difficult times.

    ★ Jesus is with us when we're tempted to do drugs or alcohol. Discuss.

- Ask each one to write a personal prayer in which they ask for awareness of Jesus' presence in a specific situation during the coming week.

IT'S A GHOST!

Luke 24:33b-43 and John 20:19-21

OBJECTIVE: To realize that things may not always be what they seem.

GETTING READY: Prepare and do the following in advance:

❑ Check to make sure the teachers taking on the Jesus, Cleopas and friend roles are available.

❑ Assign teachers to the roles of disciples and others in Jerusalem.

❑ Plan a practice session for those who will pantomime the story.

❑ Place a table and chairs center front and set a lighted candle on it.

❑ On back of the EMMAUS poster, print JERUSALEM and place on easel.

❑ Teachers, according to grades are given suggestions for planning their class time, listed below.

A. ASSEMBLY:

1. Individual teachers sit near the aisle, next to their children.

2. A disciple, hunched over, looking fearfully from side to side, slips in and sits at the table. Head on hands. Others come in from all sides; their furtive glances show their fear (John 20:19). Each simulates opening and closing a door as they come in. The last one forgets and first disciple anxiously motions for him or her to close it. With facial expressions, hand motions and walking back and forth, they portray their grief and fear.

3. Cleopas and friend run down the aisle, pound on the door, and excitedly pantomime the good news. Use motions like drawing the cross in the air, pushing it down and rolling away the stone. They create a big circle with arms and look up in joy. They take bread from the table, bless and eat it in Jesus' manner, nodding and smiling. The disciples shake their heads and show disapproval and disbelief. (*Move out of pantomime.*)

4. Jesus appears and they all cry out, "It's a ghost!" They cringe in fear. Jesus says, "Don't be afraid, it is I!" He shows them the marks on hands and feet and says, "Touch me. I'm real!" Hesitantly they move forward. Jesus says, "Do you have anything to eat?" One hands him food and all eagerly bend forward to watch him eat.

A disciple calls out, "It's Jesus Christ, it's not a ghost." Others chime in and chant the words repeatedly. They form a circle around Jesus, arms on each others shoulders and move rhythmically, chanting the words. The circle opens up and disciples beckon children and teachers to join them. The circle around Jesus expands until everyone in the room is a part of it and all chant.

5. A disciple leads out in stanzas 1-3 of, "It's Jesus Christ, Hallelujah!" (EXHIBIT A-3). Others join in and continue to sing. Jesus moves down the aisle, leading a procession. Two disciples, holding hands with each other and those behind them, follow. They may walk or dance with joy. All become part of this human chain that moves singing down the hallway to the classrooms.

B. CLASSROOM

PRE-SCHOOL TO KINDERGARTEN

Materials needed:

❑ floor map with footsteps remaining as last Sunday.

❑ Halloween mask.

❑ eight 2"x2" pieces of wood cut into 6" lengths.

❑ marking pens.

❑ teacher's and student's smile faces (*see First Sunday*).

Preparation:

❑ Draw faces on two sides of the wood, one side serious, the other side joyful. Cleopas and friend have only smiles. Face of Jesus is friendly. Jesus figure wears a hood to differentiate him from the others.

❑ Learn the song, "Praise Him, Praise Him." (EXHIBIT B-1)

Time with the children:

• Teacher welcomes the children. Walk on the map with them, first to JERUSALEM, then to EMMAUS and back to JERUSALEM. Say, "Remember, Cleopas and his friend ran to Jerusalem. They're still there. Today we'll see what happens next."

• While children move into a circle and sit down, put on the Halloween mask. Ask, "Who am I?" Let them respond. Some will respond with what they see. Now ask, "Who am I, really?" Help them differentiate between the mask and the real you.

• Tell this short story:

> It was Halloween. Kenny and his mom filled a bowl with candy bars. The doorbell rang. Two ghosts and a pumpkin stood at the door. "Trick or treat," they called. Mommy smiled and gave them candy. Kenny stared and stared. He was only two and a half years old. He had never seen trick or treaters.
>
> "Don't be scared, Kenny," said the pumpkin. She took off her green leaf mask. It's me Susan." It was the girl next door. Kenny laughed.
>
> "Mommy, I want to go too. I want to go to Chad's house." He drew on cardboard with markers. His mom cut out eyes and a mouth and attached a string. They walked to Chad's house. Kenny wore his mask. He carried an orange bag. He pushed the doorbell. Chad's mom opened the door.

"Tricky treaky," Kenny called.

"Oooh," Chad's mom said, acting scared. Are you a monster?"

"No," he laughed and pulled off his mask. "I'm Kenny." She gave him a little sack of candy. "I'm glad it's you, Kenny," she said.

- Briefly mention that sometimes we get scared of something because we don't know what it is. Allow a few moments for their feedback. Now say, "That happened to Jesus' friends one night. Remember when Cleopas and his friend met Jesus? When Jesus came to their house? Remember the big surprise? This visitor was not a stranger, it was Jesus. Jesus was alive! Remember how happy they were?"

- Sing the last stanza of the song (*see Third Sunday*).

   "It's our dear friend, Je-sus. It's our dear friend, Je-sus,

   "What a big sur-prise. What a big sur-prise.

- Arrange the wooden characters and move them around as you tell this story:

   "It was night. A pale moon looked down from the sky. Stars twinkled. Cleopas said. "We have to go to Jerusalem to tell all the friends that we saw Jesus."

   "It's bedtime," said his friend. "It's dark outside."

   "I'm not scared," said Cleopas. "We <u>must</u> go" Cleopas and his friend didn't have a car. They had no horse. No bus. They walked. They ran. Faster and faster. Finally they saw the sign, JERUSALEM." They found the house. Cleopas looked through the window. He saw their friends. He knocked.

   "Who's there," said a frightened voice.

   "It's us," Cleopas shouted. "We saw Jesus, he's alive." Slowly, the door opened. "He's alive," Cleopas said again. But the friends said, "No, No. You've had a dream. He can't be alive. No. No."

   They heard footsteps. They looked. There was Jesus.

   "Oh, oh," they cried. "It's ghost. It's a ghost."

   "No," said Jesus. "I'm not a ghost. It's me. I'm real." He ate some fish. They touched his hands. It was Jesus, not a ghost.

- Sing the following song several times (to the tune of Happy Birthday).

   We're happy it's you. We're happy it's you.
   We're happy dear Jesus. We're so happy it's you.

- Sing "Praise Him, Praise Him," using the traditional melody or one with simpler melody and pitch for young voices. (EXHIBIT B-1). All hold up their smile faces as they sing.

PRIMARY

Materials needed:

- ❑ floor map with footsteps remaining as last Sunday.
- ❑ various colors of construction paper.
- ❑ scissors, markers and heavy string or shoelaces.
- ❑ Bible story book with some pictures.
- ❑ dried beans.
- ❑ good quality white paper and colored chalk.
- ❑ a 9"x13" cake pan half filled with water.
- ❑ clothesline and clothespins.

Preparation:

- ❑ Learn the song, "Praise Him, Praise Him." (EXHIBIT B-1)
- ❑ Learn the Bible story so you can tell it using eye contact.
- ❑ Lay string and scissors beside the construction paper.
- ❑ Place paper, chalk and pan in the center of the table.
- ❑ Attach the clothesline to two sides of the room.

Time with the children:

- As the children arrive, ask them to walk on the map, first to JERUSALEM, then to EMMAUS and back to JERUSALEM. Say, "Remember, Cleopas and his friend ran to Jerusalem. They're still there. Today we'll see what happens next."

- Move into a circle. Say, "Cleopas and his friend were very happy. They felt like jumping and dancing. They felt like running and hopping. Why were they happy?"

- Engage in some happy time activities:

  - ★Sing, "Praise Him, Praise Him," using the traditional melody or this one with simpler melody and pitch for younger voices. (EXHIBIT B-1) Stand and do these actions: Phrase 1, raise arms high. Phrase 2, point to others. Phrase 3, hands over heart. (*If you sing additional stanzas, make up actions accordingly.*)

  - ★Join in a HAPPY MARCH around the room, clapping and marching as all sing the last stanza of the song (*see Third Sunday*).

    "It's our dear friend, Je-sus. It's our dear friend, Je-sus,
    "What a big sur-prise. What a big sur-prise.

- A game: Move to the table. Each child makes a mask from construction paper, using markers and scissors. Attach string and put them on. Give each one three beans. Ask them to mingle and do the following: A child asks another, "Who am I?" If the other guesses the name, he/she collects a bean from her. If the guess is wrong, he/she must give up a bean. Set a time limit.

Children count their beans when through. The one with the most beans, collects the masks. Children return to the circle.

- Ask, "Did most of you know each other? Did the masks fool you? Sometimes things are not what they really seem to be. You see a little boy screaming and crying. He fell off the swing. You run to help him. But he's only scared. He doesn't even have a scratch." Use a few other examples of situations where what we see may not be the real thing.

- Note that Cleopas and his friend saw Jesus but thought he was a stranger. How happy they were when they found out who it really was. "Today's story continues from last time. Now some other friends of Jesus are fooled. They even think he's a ghost." Tell the story, pointing to the figures in the story book (or ask children to point them out.)

- Sing the following song (to the tune of Happy Birthday).

  We're happy it's you. We're happy it's you.
  We're happy dear Jesus. We're so happy it's you.

- Return to the table and suggest they draw a picture about the story using colored chalk. Ask that they also put themselves into the scene. Raise questions such as, "If you were there, where would you be? What would you do? What would you say?" Dip the paper sheets into water and lay one down for each child. When finished, pin to clothesline. Ask, "Would you like to tell us about your picture? Take a few moments to share. Talk about Jesus being with us even if we can't see him. On a simple level, share how Jesus comes to us through others. Jesus is alive. He's with us.

- Sing stanzas 1-3 of "It's Jesus Christ, Hallelujah!." (EXHIBIT A-3)

JUNIOR

Materials needed:

❑ map of Palestine and New Testaments.

❑ paper and pencils.

❑ art prints or pictures depicting Jesus (search old curriculum picture files or go the the library).

❑ Leo Tolstoy's story "Where Love Is, There God Is Also." (EXHIBIT B-2)

Preparation:

❑ Lay out markers and other map materials.

❑ Study the story according to Luke 24:33b-43.

❑ Have ready art prints or pictures depicting Jesus.

❑ Read Tolstoy or read the abbreviated version (EXHIBIT B-2) and outline the story in 10 points—make copies.

❑ Make Parent Permission slips (see PLANNING AHEAD at end of lesson).

Time with the students:

- As students arrive, move to the map. Ask them where today's story took place. Note that last week, the two were running back to Jerusalem. They're still there. Note that the two are retracing their steps—from Emmaus back to Jerusalem. Suggest they circle the word JERUSALEM to remind them where the scene takes place. Review #7, #6 and #5. Jesus came from _____ before #5? Direct them to #4 on the map. Help them identify the name of the place and what occurred there during Jesus' ministry. Students mark the place on the map and connect it to #5 with the road.

- Divide the class into three groups and assign the Scripture lesson to each one. Give them 10 minutes to read it. Groups 1-2 list as many, WHY? questions as they can. For example, "Why were Cleopas and his friend in such a hurry?" (*Note the urgency and excitement in vs. 34-35 created by the use of long sentences.*) Group 3 looks for and writes down the verbs in this passage.

- Note that today's story is still a continuation of last week. This is a second sighting. It's a ghost story. If this were a Halloween ghost story, what would it sound like? Sit in a circle and tell a group ghost story, based on the information in Luke 24:36-42. One person starts, says a few sentences and when he or she stops, the person to the left must continue. Excitement is added if they stop in mid-sentence or at a climactic point. Stop the story at an appropriate time by calling out, "The end!" Discuss, "How was your story different from the one in Luke?"

- Now discuss the WHY? questions. Also discuss how the verbs and sentences used help describe the mood of the scene.

- "Would you recognize Jesus if he showed up in your house or at your dinner table? For centuries artists have tried to paint Jesus. Which of these would you say is Jesus?" Show the art prints of Jesus which you collected. Discuss.

- Ask, "How do we recognize Jesus? How does Jesus come to us? When we see another person, is it just a person or do we see Jesus? (Matthew 25:35-36). State what the great Russian writer, Leo Tolstoy believed. Hand out the 10 point sheets. Tell Tolstoy's story based on these points. Reflect, "Things are not always what they seem. Think of ways Jesus may come to us during this week, not as a ghost but as the risen Lord." Encourage them to reflect on this as you close with silent prayer.

Planning Ahead With The Junior Class:

- The upcoming theme for two weeks from today (*sixth Sunday*) explores ways to care about others. Invite the class to your home that day for lunch or a snack. Plan to bake and package low calorie dove-shaped cookies (*Pentecost*) for the elderly. Contact your local nursing home and arrange for your students to present the cookies and a brief program at a suitable time. Because transportation may be involved, be sure to pass out Parent Permission slips to be signed during the week and returned next Sunday.

SEEING IS BELIEVING

John 20:24-28

OBJECTIVE: To respond to happy surprises.

GETTING READY: Prepare and do the following in advance:

❑ Check to make sure the teacher taking on the Jesus role is available.

❑ Assign a teacher to the Thomas role.

❑ Make a paper head band for Thomas, with his name on it.

❑ Assign teachers (*who can sing*) to the roles of disciples.

❑ Hang a horizontal newsprint banner across the front with large lettering, DISCIPLES MEETING, printed on it.

❑ Place JERUSALEM sign on easel.

❑ Make a sign that says, ONE WEEK LATER.

❑ Prepare familiar songs/hymns of praise for all to sing.

❑ Write the responsive reading, *NOW I BELIEVE,* on newsprint and attach to the wall.

❑ Let all teachers know in advance that they are to join in the Lord's Prayer when the disciples recite it and in any familiar songs.

❑ Teachers, according to grades are given suggestions for planning their class time, listed below.

A. ASSEMBLY

1. Individual teachers sit near the aisle, next to their children.

2. The disciples walk in from different parts of the room. The first one kneels in silent prayer. Others come in and also kneel, forming a semi-circle. Facial expressions show emotion and joy. After a few moments of silent prayer, they slowly raise their arms and recite the Lord's Prayer in unison. Teachers and children join in.

3. Disciples rise, face the children and sing praise songs such as, "Praise God from Whom all Blessings Flow," "Praise Him, Praise Him," and others. As they sing, Thomas walks in. Seems surprised. Asks, "Why are you so happy? Our Lord is dead and you're happy? What's going on?" They tell him.

Thomas shakes his head in disbelief and let's them know they're talking nonsense. "They assure him, "But we all saw him, we touched him, we watched him eat. He's alive."

Thomas shouts, "No, it's not true. It can't be. The only way, I'll believe it is if I can touch him and see for myself!"

4. Thomas puts the sign ONE WEEK LATER on the easel, joins the group and all freeze for about 30 seconds.

Jesus walks in, stretches his hand out and says, "Peace be with you." He walks towards Thomas and invites him to touch him. Thomas clutches Jesus' hands, falls on his knees and cries out, "My Lord and my God!" Disciples gather around Jesus, and joyfully sing stanza 1, "It's Jesus Christ, Hallelujah!" (EXHIBIT A-3). They motion the children to sing with them. Thomas steps forward and invites the group to join in the responsive reading:

Now I Believe

Thomas:	Now I believe! Behold I bring you news of great joy Which shall be to all people. Christ is risen indeed!
Response:	Glory to God in the highest And on earth peace. Christ is risen indeed!

5. Thomas and disciples sing stanzas 4-5, It's "Jesus Christ, Halleluiah!" (EXHIBIT A-3) two times. They invite the children to sing with them the second time. They exit down center aisle, singing the stanzas again.

The children follow, singing. Jesus comes last, and waves at children as they enter their rooms.

PRE-SCHOOL TO KINDERGARTEN

Materials needed:

❑ floor map with footsteps remaining as last Sunday.

❑ a Surprise Box containing small trinkets.

Preparation:

❑ Prepare to tell the Kenny story.

❑ Decorate a box and buy trinkets to put into it.

❑ Learn the actions that accompany the Thomas story.

Time with the children:

• Teacher welcomes the children. Walk on the map with them, first to JERUSALEM, then to EMMAUS and back to JERUSALEM. Say, "We have been in Jerusalem with Cleopas and his friends. Today, we are still in Jerusalem."

• Sit in a circle. Tell this story:

70

Mom went to the mailbox to get the paper. Kenny stood at the window and watched her. She walked back to the house. Kenny waited and waited. Mom didn't come in. He waited some more. Where was she? He heard a funny noise at the door. He ran to the door. There was the noise again. It sounded like a fuzzy, faraway voice. "Kenny, Kenny."

"Who is it?" Kenny asked.

"It's Mom, please open the door."

"You don't sound like Mom!"

"I forgot my keys. Get a chair and put your eye to the little hole in the door. You'll see it's your Mom."

Kenny looked. He saw a red shirt and brown, curly hair. It was Mom.

He opened the door. Mommy hugged him. "I'm glad it's you," Kenny said.

Talk about the story, using questions like, "Kenny didn't think the noise was Mom's voice. Why not?" "What did Kenny say, when he saw it was Mom?"

Here's another happy surprise story:

"Thomas couldn't believe his ears (*hands over ears*). His friends said, "Jesus is alive. We saw him."

"No, no," said Thomas, (*shake head*) "I don't believe you."

"But it's true," said his friends (nodding).

"No, no," said Thomas, (*shake head*) "If I can touch his hands, (*hold hands together*) then I'll know he's real." His friends laughed (*laugh*). His friends smiled, (*smile*). They all went to bed (*cheek on hands*). They fell asleep (*close eyes*).

One day Thomas and his friends heard a voice (*hands behind ears*) near the door. "Peace," said the voice. Thomas looked up (*look up*). Where had he heard that voice before?

"Thomas come and touch my hands," said the man (*beckon*). He came closer (*shift forward*). Now Thomas knew who it was. It was Jesus. What a happy surprise! (*clap hands*)

- Sing and clap this stanza *(see Third Sunday)* several times. Note the word change.

  It's my dear friend, Jesus. It's my dear friend, Jesus.
  What a big surprise. What a big surprise.

- Ask, "Do you like happy surprises?" Bring out the Surprise Box. Ask questions like, "You can't see what's in it, can you hear what's in it?" (*shake the box and let them guess*) "You can't hear what's in it, can you smell what's in it?" (*let them sniff and guess*) "You can't smell what's in it, can you feel what's in it?" Let them explore with their hands and guess. Now let each one take out a trinket. Surprise?

- Say, "Thomas was very surprised and very happy. He knew Jesus was alive. He knew Jesus was with him. And we know Jesus is with us."

- Sing the following song several times *(to the tune of Happy Birthday)*.

71

We're happy it's you. We're happy it's you.
We're happy, dear Jesus. We're so happy it's you.

We like this surprise. We like this surprise.
We love our friend, Jesus. And we like this surprise.

PRIMARY

Materials needed;

❑ squares of white and black felt.

❑ scissors and glue.

❑ masking tape.

❑ old shoe, bottles, glasses, small books, cups, etc.

❑ pastel-colored candy Easter eggs or jelly beans.

Preparation:

❑ Cut different sizes circles from the white felt and glue small black circles in the center of each one.

❑ Double up masking tape and attach to the back of the eye.

❑ Stack the shoes, bottles, etc. on the center of the table.

❑ Hide the candy eggs or put pastel-colored jelly beans into net squares, tie with a ribbon and hide.

❑ Make arrangements for your children to visit someone who is homebound, in two weeks *(seventh Sunday)*. (See FRIENDS FOR JESUS at the end of this lesson.)

❑ Make Parent Permission slips and hand them out.

Time with the children:

• As the children arrive, ask them to walk on the map, first to JERUSALEM, then to EMMAUS and back to JERUSALEM. Say, "Cleopas and his friend ran to Jerusalem to tell their friends that Jesus was alive. Today, we are still in Jerusalem. Let's see what happens next."

• Create a setting. Say, "Sometimes we don't believe something until we can see it or touch it *(develop the idea and get their input)*. And when it's true, it's a big surprise! That's what happened to Thomas."

• Note that there were a number of friends gathered at the house in Jerusalem. We don't know who they were. We know they were Jesus' friends and some of his disciples. These friends had seen Jesus but Thomas hadn't.

• Suggest they pretend to be friends and disciples. Each one thinks of a name to give him/herself and then selects an item from the table that best describes what that person is like. Allow them to select from your group of eyes and show them how to attach them to their selected item. Select two items

72

to represent Thomas and Jesus. Hold Thomas and Jesus in your right and left hands and have them act according to the script.

- Tell the following story. Pause at the blanks, so the selected child can make his or her eye puppet nod and call out, "WE SAW HIM." Do this as often as you wish and with as many children as you wish to help involve them in the story.

> "Thomas didn't believe his friends. He didn't believe, (*point to a child*) who said, "_____ " (*Child holds up eye puppet and makes it nod as he or she calls out, "WE SAW HIM." Repeat with several children.*)
>
> "No, no," said Thomas, "It's not true." (*Teacher's eye puppet shakes head.*)
>
> "But," said _____(*point to a child*), it's true," _____. (*Child repeats action and words indicated above. Repeat with several children.*)
>
> "No, no," said Thomas, (*Teacher's puppet shakes head.*) "If I can see him and touch his hands, then I'll believe what you say.
>
> _____(*Point to a child*) smiled and said, _____(*repeat*).
>
> _____(*Point to a child*) gave a happy laugh and said,_____ (*repeat*).
>
> One day Thomas and his friends heard a voice near the door. "Peace," said the voice. Thomas looked up. (*Teacher uses appropriate puppet actions.*)
>
> "Thomas, come and touch my hands," said the man. He came closer. (*Teacher moves Jesus puppet.*) Now Thomas knew who it was. It was Jesus. Now everybody said (*include Thomas*) " What a happy surprise!"

- Sing stanzas 1 and 4 of, "It's Jesus Christ, Hallelujah!" (Exhibit A-3).

- Note that the class will now have a happy surprise. Give them a color hint of what they're looking for and allow them to hunt for the candy. When all have found some (*help them if necessary*) sit around the table. Note that the egg is a sign of new life and reminds us that Jesus is alive. That was a happy surprise for Thomas. Let's remember the happy surprise, Jesus loves us and is with us.

- After you have eaten, sing "Praise Him, Praise Him" (Exhibit B-1) with actions (*see Fourth Sunday*).

FRIENDS FOR JESUS. Note that two weeks from today (*seventh Sunday*) the lesson will be on sharing the good news with others. How can we do that? One way is to meet with our class in the home of someone who can't come to church because of age or disability. That's what the class will do in two weeks time. *(This may be done during the regular session time or later that day. See Sixth Sunday, FRIENDS FOR JESUS.)*

Talk about ways to bring good news to that person. 1) Have a short Sunday School time together with the host. 2) Give some gifts. Suggest they bring small, packaged gifts next Sunday. They will put numbers on them, present them when they visit the home and suggest he or she open one each day during the next weeks, beginning with #1. 3) Sing some songs.

Hand out Parent Permission slips and note they are to be returned next Sunday or by mail.

JUNIOR:

Materials needed:

- ❑ map of Palestine and New Testaments.
- ❑ paper and pencils.
- ❑ chalkboard and chalk.
- ❑ candy bars for a surprise treat.

Preparation:

- ❑ Lay out markers and other map materials.
- ❑ Study the story according to John 20:24-28.
- ❑ Plan the court session suggested in material.
- ❑ Write the outline for the PRAISE acrostic on the chalkboard.
- ❑ Collect Parent Permission slips.

Time with the students:

As students arrive, move towards the map. Ask them where today's story took place. Note that last week they were in the house of the disciples and friends in Jerusalem. They're still there. Suggest they draw another circle around Jerusalem to remind them where the scene takes place. It also helps them see that most of these final sightings occur in and near Jerusalem. Review the post resurrection events to date. Review #7, #6, #5, and #4. Jesus came from _____ before #4? Direct them to #3 on the map. Help them identify the name of the place and what occurred there during Jesus' ministry. Students mark the place on the map and connect it to #4 with the road.

- Note that this is the third 'sighting' after Easter morning—this time by a man who needed proof to believe. Assign the Scripture lesson to the students. Ask them to read it quietly and list the most important events on paper. Now ask them to write a 10-line story of what happened in their own words. Share the stories.

- Set up a courtroom scene with a judge, jury, witnesses, prosecutor, defense lawyers and Thomas the defendant. Thomas, a federal agent, stands accused of giving false information to the FBI and leaking it to the press. He has told a reporter that a man, Jesus, who was a threat to government security and therefore executed, is alive. Not only has Thomas leaked that information (*which may or may not be true*) but there is suspicion that he may be a double agent; that he is not faithful to the national government, but a spy for, and a key member of a radical, subversive group (*the Kingdom of God*).

    With this in mind, determine roles that each one may play and conduct a hearing. Call on witnesses, and if necessary, put Thomas on the stand. How does the jury find him?

★ In all likelihood, the jury will find Thomas "not guilty." Even if they find him guilty, no one can steal the joy of Thomas, because he believes that what he saw is true. Say, "Make the joy of Thomas your joy. Write the letters PRAISE vertically on the board and create an acrostic Psalm of Praise with the class (each sentence starts with consecutive letters P... R... A... I... S... E...). When finished, read it in unison.

★ Note that the story of Thomas includes two ways of faith: 1) Faith that can't believe until there is proof. 2) Faith that believes even if there is no proof. Discuss the everyday events we believe in that we know are true because we have proof. For example, we believe we won't get stuck in mud on a major highway because it is paved, we can reach the moon because astronauts have done so, etc. Get their input. Also note that there are many things we believe even without proof. For example we believe that the universe is endless, that after winter comes spring, an electronic message will reach its destination, that our friend is faithful, that our parents love us, etc. Discuss.

★ Note that all the 'sighting' stories after the resurrection contained proof of the resurrection (*appearances and eating bread, eating fish, and seeing/touching*). We only have their word for it so we believe without seeing. But Jesus comes to us through friends, family, good times and happy surprises. Wherever there is a happy surprise, we like Thomas, can praise God, because we know Jesus is there. Life is full of happy, God-surprises.

- Bring out candy bars as a surprise treat. As they eat, plug into their responses as you talk about God's surprises.

Planning Ahead With The Junior Class:

Review the theme of caring about others, scheduled for next week (*sixth Sunday*). Work on some of the advance details. Collect the Parent Permission slips.

LET'S EAT!

John 21:1-17

OBJECTIVE: To explore ways to care about others.

GETTING READY: Prepare and do the following in advance:

- ❑ Check to make sure the teacher taking on the Jesus role is available.
- ❑ Assign teachers to the disciple and Peter roles.
- ❑ Circle the room with blue crepe paper streamers, to represent a lake.
- ❑ Make a sign, SEA OF GALILEE (Tiberius) and place on easel located inside the blue crepe paper circle.
- ❑ Cut and pass out construction paper fish to all children (*to simulate being fishing disciples on the lake*).
- ❑ Teachers, according to grades are given suggestions for planning their class time, listed below.

A. ASSEMBLY:

1. Individual teachers sit near the aisle, next to their children.

2. Jesus walks in carrying a fruit platter. He turns and gives a brief monologue to the children:

> Three years ago I walked to the Sea of Galilee. Peter and his partners, James and John were fishing. I said, "Go to the deep water and catch some fish." Peter said, "We fished all night and caught no fish but if you say so, we'll try again." They did. Soon both boats were filled. Peter said, "I'm sorry I didn't believe you." I said, "Don't worry. From now on you will catch people for God."

> Now, it's three years later. Shortly after Easter. I'm at the same lake again. Peter and six other disciples are fishing. I call out, "Children, have you any fish?" "No," they call back. "Try again on the right side of your boat," I call. They do. The boat is soon full. I make a fire on the shore, and cook some fish and bread. Then I call out, "Coms on. Let's eat breakfast!."

3. A disciple cries out from the back of the room, "It's the Lord!" Peter rushes down the aisle shouting, "Yes, it's the Lord!" He starts singing stanza 1, "It's Jesus Christ. Hallelujah!" (EXHIBIT A-3) and beckons the children to join him. Sing several times. Peter indicates that all in the room are disciples on the lake and invites them to come ashore for a snack. Jesus says, "Bring some more fish." The children come forward and give their paper fish to Jesus. Peter helps Jesus serve the fruit.

4. Peter hushes the children as they stand around and eat their fruit. He talks to them:
I felt unhappy. You know why? When Jesus was on trial, I was scared. I thought they might get me too. So when someone asked, "You're one of Jesus' followers, aren't you?" I said, "I don't know the man!" Three times this happened. I thought I'd never forgive myself. What about Jesus? Would he ever forgive me? You know what happened? After eating, he took me aside. He made me feel special. "Do you love me more than anything or anyone?" he asked. "O, yes, Lord," I said. "Then take care of my lambs, my little ones. Share the good news with the boys and girls." Again he asked, "Do you love me?" "Yes, yes," I said. And again he asked,"Do you love me? Take care of my sheep, the big people. Share the good news with everyone," he said. I knew now that I would follow Jesus the rest of my life. And I knew he had forgiven me.

Peter invites the children to sing, "I Have Decided" (EXHIBIT B-3) or "I Have Decided to Follow Jesus" Sing and Rejoice. Newton, KS: Faith and Life Press, 1979, #39, as he leads them across the lake, into the hallway towards their classrooms.

PRE-SCHOOL TO KINDERGARTEN

Materials needed:

❑ floor map with footsteps leading to the Sea of Galilee.

❑ a dark colored sheet.

❑ cottonballs, cardboard and lamb patterns.

❑ glue, eyes (*from craft shop*)

Preparation:

❑ Mark SEA OF GALILEE in distant corner of room and extend the footsteps.

❑ Prepare to tell the fishing story.

❑ Lay the blanket in the circle area to represent a boat.

❑ Cut out cardboard lambs for all children.

❑ Make one demonstration lamb, gluing on cotton balls and the eyes.

Time with the children:

• Teacher welcomes the children. Walk on the map with them, first to EMMAUS and then back to JERUSALEM. Say, "Today we have to walk many miles to a lake. Jesus friends are fishing in the lake." Walk to the SEA OF GALILEE sign.

• Tell this involvement story:

Peter, Jesus' disciple and his friends got into their boats. Let's pretend we are Peter's friends. (*Tell them the sheet is a boat. Invite them to sit in two rows on it, facing you*). They rowed to the middle of the lake (*all row*). They fished and fished (*cast and pull in*). They heard a voice (*hands behind ears*). They saw Jesus on the shore (*hands shading eyes*). They rowed back to shore (*all row*). Peter was so excited, he jumped in and swam (*teacher gets up and swims*). They all got to shore (*get out of boat*) They were glad to see Jesus. (*clap hands*)

- Form a circle, holding hands and walk around as all sing the following (*see Third Sunday*) several times. Note the word change.

    It's our dear friend, Jesus. It's our dear friend Jesus,
    What a nice surprise. What a nice surprise.

- Move to the table. Say, "Jesus and his disciple friends ate breakfast. Yummy. Yummy. Then Jesus said to Peter, "I want to have a word with you. Alone." Jesus asked, "Do you love me?" Peter said (*children respond, "Yes!" several times in chorus*). " Then," said Jesus, "take care of my little lambs; the little boys and girls."

- Note that Jesus wants us to take care of and be friends with other boys and girls too. Also our brothers and sisters. Talk about ways we can care about others. Show them the lamb and help them each make one. Then talk about sharing their lambs and who they will give them to.

- Sing the following song several times (*to the tune of Happy Birthday*).

    We're glad to be friends. We're glad to be friends.
    We care about others, and we're glad to be friends.

PRIMARY

Materials needed:

- ❑ floor map with footsteps leading to the Sea of Galilee.
- ❑ newsprint and blue markers.
- ❑ file cards and felt tip pen.
- ❑ heart patterns, red construction paper, lace and trimmings.
- ❑ glue, scissors, markers.

Preparation:

- ❑ Mark SEA OF GALILEE in distant corner of room and extend the footsteps.
- ❑ Write consecutive numbers on file cards for as many cards as there are children.
- ❑ Prepare to present the story of Jesus and the disciples.
- ❑ Draw a large circle, to represent the lake, on newsprint.
- ❑ Cut out heart patterns for all the children.
- ❑ Make red decorated hearts for all children.

Time with the children:

- As the children arrive, ask them to walk on the map, first to JERUSALEM, then to EMMAUS and back to JERUSALEM. Say, "Today we have to walk many miles to a lake. Jesus' friends are fishing in the lake." Walk to the SEA OF GALILEE sign. "Now, let's see what happens next."

- Sit in a circle around the newsprint lake (the Sea of Galilee). Say, "Today we're going to have a Spot Story." Pass out the numbered file cards. Note that as you tell the story, you will call out a number. The child with that number takes the blue marker and puts many or few dots on or beside the lake (*to represent people, fish, lambs and sheep, as indicated by the story. Change or repeat the numbers according to how many children there are in your class.*) Now tell this story:

  > Peter, John and five other disciples went fishing on the Sea of Galilee. (Call #1). They fished and fished (#2). They caught many fish (#3). They caught more fish (#4). Jesus walked to the lake and stood on the shore (#5). He saw the disciples on the lake (#6). Jesus made a fire and cooked fish and bread (#7). "Come and eat," he called (8). "It's the Lord," John called. Peter jumped into the lake and swam to shore (#9). The others came and they all ate breakfast (#10).

  > Jesus had a special talk with Peter (#11). "I love you more than anything in the world," Peter said. Three times he said this (#12). "Then," said Jesus, "I want you to take care of my lambs and my sheep—the little children and the big people. I want you to love them and share the good news of God's love with them. Wherever you go. (*Instruct all children to cover the lake and surrounding area with dots to represent the many children and people.*)

- Sing and clap the following (*see Third Sunday*). Note word change.

  > *Peter said, "I'll do it." Peter said, "I will do it.*
  > *I will feed your lambs. I will feed your sheep."*

- Note that Jesus wants us to take care of and be friends with others too. Being friends is a way of sharing the good news that God loves us. We can show love to and share with other boys and girls, our brothers and sisters, mom's and dads and many other special people. How? Talk about ways we can care about others. Hand out the hearts you made for them and indicate it's one way you can say, "I love you, God loves you."

- Pass out the heart patterns, paper and other materials and ask each one to make a special heart. Talk about who they may want to give this heart too. Sing the following song several times (to the tune of Happy Birthday).

  > *We're glad to be friends. We're glad to be friends.*
  > *We care about others, and we're glad to be friends.*

FRIENDS FOR JESUS: Talk about where you will be going for class next week (*Seventh Sunday*) and plan the details. Because of the time limit, you may prefer not to attend ASSEMBLY and use the full hour. If you choose to make your visit later that day, use the class session as a rehearsal time. Plan to repeat most of the same lesson when you make your visit. Today, collect Parent Permission slips. Also collect the gifts they brought. Children put numbers on the gifts.

JUNIOR:

Materials needed:

- ❑ floor map and markers.
- ❑ map of Palestine and New Testaments.
- ❑ paper and pencils.
- ❑ cookie recipes.
- ❑ small gift boxes, wrapping paper, scissors, glue and ribbons.

Preparation:

- ❑ Lay out markers and other map materials.
- ❑ Study the story according to John 21:1-17
- ❑ Plan details for the class's visit to your home. Purchase groceries for baking cookies and several dove-shaped cookie cutters.
- ❑ Collect small boxes, ribbons and wrapping paper for packing individual cookie gifts.
- ❑ Initiate some ideas for a brief program the children may wish to present at the Nursing Home.
- ❑ Double check the schedule for visiting the Nursing Home and finalize transportation.

Time with the students:

- As students arrive, direct them to the map. Ask them where today's story took place. Note that last week they were in Jerusalem with Thomas and the disciples. To date all the 'sightings' recorded have been in Judaea. Now the Gospel of John takes us north to Galilee. Ask if they can recall any other events that took place on the Sea of Galilee during Jesus' ministry (*calling of disciples, draught of fishes, stilling of the storm, walking on water*). Students mark in THE SEA OF GALILEE and connect it to JERUSALEM. Review the post resurrection events todate. Review #7, 6, 5, 4 and 3. Jesus came from _____ before #3. Direct them to #2 on the map. Help them identify the name of the place and what occurred there during Jesus' ministry. Students mark the place on the map and connect it to #3 with the road.

- Introduce the story. The class reads the scripture in unison. Ask, "What are the main events here? Who are the main actors?" Note that today's theme has to do with caring. Jesus showed his love and care for the disciples in two ways. Ask if they can identify these. (1. Cooking and serving a meal. 2. Expressing love, concern and forgiveness to Peter). Care for others is demonstrated through both action and words. Discuss what this means for their lives.

- Note that three out of four 'sightings' after the resurrection have to do with eating together. The early church shared meals, ate together and celebrated the Lord's Supper regularly. They believed that in eating together, sharing food and conversation, Christ made himself known. Talk about ways we can

80

practice hospitality, friendship and caring to others. Discuss how we see Jesus in others and how others see Jesus in us.

- Carry your discussion over to plans for the afternoon. Talk about eating together at your home and the significance of Jesus being present. Discuss the plans to make cookies. Note that it's important to cut the sugar content in half because many elderly must limit sugar in their diet. Plan how to package and decorate.

PROGRAM: Relate your program to the themes you have been studying. Consider some of the following:

a) Read the scripture from one of the stories.
b) Present a synopsis of one of the skits used during assembly.
c) Use the *Response of Praise*, (Easter Sunday), Thomas' affirmation of faith, *Now I Believe* (fifth Sunday) or the *Praise Acrostic* (fifth Sunday).
d) Consider sharing learning, experiences from the class sessions.
e) Make posters or banners and present them.
f) Sing some of the songs sung or learned during these sessions.

When all details have been planned, form a circle and speak sentence prayers where they express concerns and care for others.

GOODBYE AND HELLO

Matthew 28:16

(Luke 24:46-53 Acts 1:8-11)

OBJECTIVE: To respond to God's love by sharing the good news.

GETTING READY: Prepare and do the following in advance:

❑ Check to make sure the teacher taking on the Jesus role is available.

❑ Assign teachers to the roles of the disciples.

❑ Ask two teachers to represent the men dressed in white.

❑ Make a sign, BETHANY and place on easel.

❑ Make a large cardboard cloud (6'x 3') fasten a handle on the back center and stand against the wall near the front.

❑ Teachers, according to grades are given suggestions for planning their class time, listed below.

A. ASSEMBLY:

1. Individual teachers sit near the aisle, next to their children.

2. Jesus walks down the aisle followed by the disciples. Jesus says, "Come to Bethany with me. I have something to tell you." The disciples sing stanzas 1-2 of "It's Jesus Christ, Hallelujah!" (EXHIBIT A-3) as they walk and motion the children to join them in singing. They kneel in a semicircle around Jesus. Jesus asks the children to kneel too. Jesus addresses the disciples and children. "I am saying goodbye. It is time for me to leave. I'm going to my Father's house. You can't come with me now, but I'm going to prepare a place for you. Later we'll be together. Always remember to love each other as I love you. Remember to share the good news of God's love, wherever you go, in Jerusalem, Judaea, Samaria and throughout the whole world. Don't be afraid. You're not alone. The Holy Spirit, whom I promised to you, will give you power and joy, and in that Spirit I will be with you always."

3. Jesus lifts his arms towards the disciples and children in an act of blessing and speaks the Numbers 6:24-26 benediction. "The Lord bless you and keep you; the Lord make his face shine upon you and be gracious to you; the Lord turn his face toward you and give you peace. Amen." He pauses then says, "Goodbye, my friends!" He turns, picks up the cloud and carries it as a shield, exiting quietly. Disciples rise and motion the children to do the same. They raise their arms, look up and sing stanzas 5-6 of "It's Jesus Christ, Halleluiah!" (EXHIBIT A-3). Children join in.

4. The two dressed in white, walk in from either side and say in unison, "Don't just stand there looking up. He'll be back. Now, you have good news to share." (*urgently*) "Go. Go. Go." Disciples turn to the children and invite them to participate in the following chant, beginning softly and getting louder each time they repeat it, until they reach a loud forte. "We have good news to share." Disciples walk down aisle and into hallways continuing the chant until all the children reach their classrooms.

B. CLASSROOM

PRESCHOOL TO KINDERGARTEN

Materials needed:

❑ floor map with footsteps leading to BETHANY.

❑ pictures of moving vans and trucks, one for each child.

❑ brightly colored sheets of paper.

❑ heart-shaped stickers and colored markers.

Preparation:

❑ Mark BETHANY on map and extend the footsteps.

❑ Make arrangements with an adult class (*possibly parents*) for Preschool and Kindergarten children to enter, sing and throw GOOD NEWS darts.

Time with the children:

- Teacher welcomes the children. Walk on the map with them, first to JERUSALEM, then to EMMAUS and back to JERUSALEM. Then walk to the SEA OF GALILEE. Say, "We have walked a long, long way. Now we must go back to where we started. A long way. Today Jesus says goodbye to his friends near a small town called BETHANY." Walk to BETHANY with them.

- Sit in a circle. Give each child a picture of a moving van. Ask some questions. Tell this story:

    Jessie and Anna packed their toys in a box. They put their shoes into a suitcase. They folded their clothes and put them into a big bag. Jessie and Anna were moving to another place. Far, far away. Jessie was happy and sad. Happy for a new home and new friends. Sad because she would miss her room and her friends.

    "I have to say goodbye to Tina," she said to Mommy. She ran to Tina's house. Tina was sad too.

    "We will talk on the telephone," Jessie promised.

    "We're coming to visit you next summer," Tina said.

    "Soon we'll be big and we can write letters," said Jessie.

    "You're my best, best friend," said Tina. "My always friend."

    "Mine too," said Jessie. "Bye friend." Tina gave Jessie a doll. Jessie gave Tina a book.

"Forever friends," said Tina.

"Forever friends," said Jessie. "Goodbye, forever friend."

Talk about friends and sometimes having to say goodbye.

- Say, "Let's go to Bethany for another goodbye story." All move back to the map. Say, "Jesus and his friends stood here like this. Jesus said, "Goodbye friends." (*all wave*) Jesus said, "I love you." (*hand over hearts*) Jesus said, "I'll be back. (*hold hands*) Jesus said, "Tell all the boys and girls the good news that God loves them." (*point to each other.*)

- Say, "We're going to share the good news of God's love with_____ this morning." (*Indicate which adult class.*) Move to the table and show them how to fold paper darts. Fold a sheet of typing paper in half, lengthwise. Fold top corner of each side to middle crease. 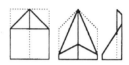 Fold the lower edge of each corner to middle crease. Bring each wing up to within 1/2 inch of middle line and fold. Fold wings back. Shape and fly. For those who can write, suggest they print GOD IS LOVE on their darts and decorate with heart stickers. Younger ones will draw on their darts with markers and put on stickers.

- When ready, rehearse the song below several times (*to the tune of Happy Birthday*), and then get ready to visit the adult class.

    God loves you and me. God loves you and me.
    The good news of Jesus, is God loves YOU and me.

    We share the good news. We share the good news.
    The good news of Jesus, yes, we share the good news.

- Walk to the adult classroom, knock on the door. Children enter and sing stanza 1 of the above song. Then they throw their GOOD NEWS darts to the adults in session. Sing stanza 2 of the song and then return to your classroom.

- Pray this short prayer together. "Thank you Jesus, for your good news. Amen."

PRIMARY.

Materials needed;

    ❏ floor map with footsteps leading to BETHANY.

    ❏ a Bible.

    ❏ a huge, round blue balloon.

    ❏ pictures of children, local and from around the world.

    ❏ glue and a long blue ribbon.

    ❏ numbered gifts for the homebound host.

Preparation:

❑ Mark BETHANY on the map and extend the footsteps.

❑ Prepare to tell the Echo Story.

❑ Look up and read, Matthew 28:16 (Acts 1:8 and Luke 24;51-52).

❑ Purchase a huge blue balloon to represent the world.

❑ Cut out numerous pictures of local children and other children from around the world.

❑ Finalize details for your class session with someone who is homebound (*Review FRIENDS FOR JESUS, fifth and sixth Sundays*).

❑ Make simple refreshments (*optional*).

Time with the children:

- Assuming you're visiting a homebound person this morning, do this before you leave: As the children arrive, ask them to walk on the map, first to JERUSALEM, then to EMMAUS, back to JERUSALEM and to the SEA OF GALILEE sign. Say, "Today we have the last story about Jesus and his friends. But it's not at the Sea of Galilee. We have to go back. We have to go for a long walk to Bethany, a small town close to Jerusalem." Walk to BETHANY.

- Once you have arrived at the home of your host, take time to introduce the children and establish a comfortable atmosphere. Together with the children, briefly tell the host about the weeks of post-resurrection stories and the way joy and excitement has been experienced. Begin by singing several of the songs you have sung during these weeks: "Jesus Loves Me," "Praise Him, Praise Him," (EXHIBIT B-1) and stanzas 1-2 of the theme song, "It's Jesus Christ Hallelujah!" (EXHIBIT A-3)

- Ask, "Have you ever said say goodbye to a special person?" Talk about it. (*Involve your host as much or as little as he or she chooses.*) "How do you feel if that special person says, "See you soon?" Note that today's story is about Jesus saying goodbye but also making the disciples very happy. Introduce the idea of an Echo Story where you say a line and they echo or repeat it back. If possible sit in a circle which incorporates the host.
  Jesus said to his disciples, (*echo*)
  "Come with me to Bethany." (*echo*)
  They walked and walked. (*echo*)
  Jesus said, "I must say goodbye." (*echo*)
  "I love you." (*echo*)
  "Love each other." (*echo*)
  "Love your family, your friends, your neighbors." (*echo*)
  "Share the good news of God's love wherever you go." (*echo*)
  "Share the good news with the whole world." (*echo*)
  "I'll see you soon." (*echo*)
  The disciples felt a little sad when Jesus left, (*echo*)
  and the disciples felt a little glad when Jesus left, (*echo*)
  because they had good, good news to tell. (*echo*)

- Say, "This is how the gospel writer Luke tells the story." Read Acts 1:8 and Luke 24:51-52. Note that the good news of God's love is to be shared everywhere. Bring out the balloon, pictures and glue. Explain that the balloon represents the world. Designate a place as local and ask children to glue pictures to that area. Be sensitive to various nationalities and races. Spread out from there with international pictures until the balloon is covered. Sing stanza 3 of "It's Jesus Christ, Hallelujah!" (EXHIBIT A-3) Attach the ribbon and present the balloon to the host.

- Note that the good news is shared in many ways, at different times and in different situations. Talk with them about where, how and when they can become bearers of good news. We also try to share good news by making others happy. We can share good news of joy with a new friend. The children present the numbered gifts and explain to the host when to open them. They invite their host to join them in stanza 7 of "It's Jesus Christ, Hallelujah!" (EXHIBIT A-3)

- If you planned refreshments, this is a good time to serve them. Close with a brief prayer.

JUNIOR:

Materials needed:

- ❑ floor map and markers.

- ❑ map of Palestine and New Testaments.

- ❑ paper and pencils.

Preparation:

- ❑ Lay out markers and other map materials.

- ❑ Study the story according to Matthew 28:16 (Luke 24:46-52 and Acts 1:8-11).

- ❑ Make final arrangements with the missionary or service speaker.

Time with the students:

- As students arrive, direct them to the map. Ask them where today's story took place. Note that last week they were at the Sea of Galilee. Today they're back in Judaea, only a few miles from Jerusalem. Students mark in BETHANY and connect it to the SEA OF GALILEE. Review #7 through #2. Jesus came from _____ before #2. Direct them to #1 on the map. Help them identify the name of the place and what occurred there during Jesus' ministry. Students mark the place on the map and connect it to #2 with the road.

- Note that historically the church has designated, Thursday, 40 days after Easter, as Ascension Day and Sunday, 50 days after Easter, as Pentecost. One could call today, Ascension Sunday. Note that this is the last 'sighting' of Jesus. Divide the class into three groups and assign one of the scripture texts to each one. Say, "You are an on-the-scene newspaper reporter from the JERUSALEM GAZETTE. In a 100 word article, describe what you see and hear. What is the main feeling expressed after Jesus leaves?" When finished, students read their news articles.

- Note that JOY is a characteristic of the gospel, the good news. The story of Jesus began with the joy of the angels and shepherds at Bethlehem. It continued with the many joy stories Jesus told and the joy of those whose lives were changed by Jesus' love. For seven Sundays, from Easter morning until now, we've heard joy stories. Note that Luke's last words are: "And they

86

returned to Jerusalem with great joy" (Luke 24:52). Why were they joyful? Why can we be joyful? What's good about the good news? (*Discuss*)

- Note that for 2000 years the good news has been shared around the world and the joy continues to spread. Introduce the guest speaker who will share about the joy of the good news in his or her place of mission or service. Close with singing stanzas 3, 6, and 7 of "It's Jesus Christ, Hallelujah!" (EXHIBIT A-3)

LET'S CELEBRATE

Acts 1:12-14, 2:14

OBJECTIVE: To celebrate the birth of the church.

GETTING READY: Prepare and do the following in advance:

❑ Assign teachers to the roles of the disciples and woman followers who will pantomime the reading and also read/recite the prayer, "Come Holy Spirit."

❑ Contact the two dressed in white (*seventh week*) to carry and hold the flame mobile.

❑ Make the flame mobile: Buy a large styrofoam ring or bend heavy wire into a circle. Wrap with red crepe paper streamers. Cut red cloth flames 12" long. Attach to ring with safety pins so flames hang down like pennants.

❑ Ask someone to read the scripture dramatically while the group pantomimes the story. (Rehearse before the session, so reading and pantomime coordinate.)

❑ Place the sign JERUSALEM on the easel.

❑ All teachers meet in advance to plan a Pentecost BIRTH OF THE CHURCH party.

❑ Make a huge birthday cake with many non-extinguishable candles on it.

❑ Purchase other supplies needed for the party and set up tables or centers where such are required.

A. ASSEMBLY:

1. Individual teachers sit near the aisle, next to their children.

2. The women walk in, form an inner semicircle and kneel in prayer.

Reader:	Acts 1:12-13. (*Disciples walk in, form a semi circle around the women and kneel.*)
Reader:	Acts 1:14. (*All read/recite the following prayer in unison:*) Come, Holy Spirit, God of love, And give us power from above, Through Jesus Christ, your only son, Grant us a love that makes us one. You are the truth, the life, the way. Help us to share that news today. Good news, good news, good news, we say,

With joyfilled hearts we kneel and pray,
Come Holy Spirit from above
And fill us with the God of love. Amen.

Reader:	Acts 2:1. (*The two in white move down the aisle carrying the flame mobile.*)
Reader:	Acts 2:2-3 (*The two stand in the center of the semicircle and hold the mobile high in the air.*)
Reader:	Acts 2:4 (*All rise and invite the children to join them in joyful dance and song.*) Sing all stanzas of "It's Jesus Christ, Hallelujah!" (EXHIBIT A-3) (*If space doesn't allow for much movement, encourage them to sway with the music, clap, or raise/wave their arms in praise.*)

3. The two in white step forward and loudly proclaim in dialogue:

#1:	The Holy Spirit, Jesus' power, started the church 2000 years ago.
#2:	That was the birth day of the church.
#1:	The Holy Spirit, Jesus' power, helps us be the church today.
#1 & #2:	The Holy Spirit, Jesus' power, helps us to love and follow Jesus.
#2:	On Pentecost Sunday, we celebrate the birthday of the church.
#1 & #2:	Today is the church's birthday. Let's all say, "Happy birthday, church!" (*They encourage the children to respond several times.*)

B. BIRTH OF THE CHURCH PARTY:

1. A leader walks in and calls out, "Let's have a party! A big birthday party!" Two carry in a huge cake aflame with candles. Others follow with punch and trays with glasses. A table is moved in and the cake placed on it. All sing the following several times to the tune of, "It's Jesus Christ, Hallelujah!" (*Note that rhythm on 'Happy' changes to 2 eighth notes.*)

> Happy birthday, church, Hallelujah!
> Happy birthday, church, Hallelujah!
> Happy birthday, church, Happy birthday, church,
> Happy birthday, church, Amen.

2. Invite some children to come forward to blow out the candles. The flames will keep coming back. Note that over the years many have tried to stop the church. But God's work cannot be defeated. Remove the candles and cut the cake. Those who participated in the pantomime help to serve.

3. Choose from any of the activities listed in Part III or do some of the following. Set up centers or activity areas to accommodate the different ages and size of groups. Suggested prizes are: age appropriate booklets, pins, pencils or other items available in religious bookstores.

A. Younger children:

1. **Gone Fishing:** Make red, yellow and blue cardboard fish and back with a magnet tape. Spread on a sheet of blue plastic to represent a pond. Tie a heavy string to a dowel and attach a washer with a magnet strip on it. Children take turns fishing. Each color of fish represents a different prize.

2. **Flag and Hat Parade:** Children cut flags from red cloth and decorate with felt pieces. Attach to a dowel. Help them fold hats from red gift wrap. Supply combs and tissue paper. Show them how to hum through the paper and make an instrument sound. To make a hat, fold a newspaper sheet in half. Fold again. Open and fold both upper corners to middle crease. Fold up about two inches from bottom. Staple ends and wear. (Use smaller sheets for smaller heads.) The children march up and down the hallway, 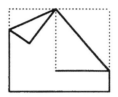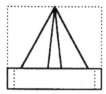 wearing their hats and waving their flags, while some of the older ones play the comb and tissue to simulate a band.

3. **Who Has the Dove?:** Buy 11 white plastic birds *(12 can play)*. Children sit in a circle. Play music on an instrument or shake a coffee can with beans in it. Pass the birds from hand to hand while making music. When the music stops, those not holding a bird are 'out.' The one going 'out' also chooses someone's bird, and takes it with him or her. The music starts again. Continue in this way until only one bird and one child are left.

4. **Good News Eggs:** Eggs continue to be the symbol of new life and the good news of the resurrection. Purchase hollow plastic eggs and put a candy in each one. Choose one into which you will also insert a small card with the words, GOOD NEWS on it. Place in a large container. Children each draw an egg. The one who draws the one with the card, receives a prize.

B. Older children:

1. **When I Go To Church I Take:** Children sit in a circle. One starts with, "When I go to church I take" *(names an item)*. The next one must repeat that item and add another one. This continues until someone misses. That person drops out. The game is over when all but one have dropped out.

2. **Pentecost Wallhanging:** On a sheet of paper list the eight post-resurrection stories they have learned about this season. Cut heavy cream colored cloth into 16" squares. Each child selects a story and designs a square with crayons, depicting a scene from the list. When finished, lay upside down on waxed paper and press with a warm iron. This fixes the crayon into the cloth. Lay them out in consecutive horizontal or vertical order. Note that these will be sewn together, a rod inserted and a string attached. The story sequence will be hung in the hallway of the education department as a reminder of the series.

3. **Sharing the Good News Relay:** Put a sign, JERUSALEM at one end of the room and a sign that reads, WORLD, at the other end. In front of WORLD, place a small table with a glass container on it. Players engage in a three legged-race, each player holding a spoon containing three pastel colored jelly beans or small Easter eggs. The new life symbol of the eggs represents the sharing of good news. Team members race from JERUSALEM to the WORLD, deposit their candy in the glass container and race back. Anyone losing candy on the way to the WORLD is 'out.' The relay is over when the first team, not losing candy, arrives back in JERUSALEM.

4. **Guess Again:** Frost 50 cookies to represent the days from Easter to Pentecost, with bright red frosting and place in a glass jar or bowl. Children sign up and guess how many cookies there are in the jar. The one who guesses closest to 50 wins a prize.

PRAISE HIM

Anonymous

Anne N. Rupp

1. Praise him, praise him, all ye lit- tle chil- dren,
2. Love him, love him, all ye lit- tle chil- dren,

God   is   love,   God   is   love.
God   is   love,   God   is   love.

TOLSTOY'S STORY

Martin the shoemaker was a lonely, bitter man. He lived in a small basement room with only one window. There he repaired shoes and watched the shoes and boots of passers-by, as they trudged past his small window. Many of them he recognized, because he had repaired, resoled and patched them as far back as he could remember. Martin did good work and the shoes he repaired lasted a long time. Neighbors would say to another, "Take your old shoes to Martin. He'll make them look like new." He did. But it didn't make him happy.

Years earlier when Martin married, he and his bride had dreams for the future. She wished for a large home and he desired a steadier income. But they were happy with what they had. Love and companionship. Understanding and sharing. When a son was born, their lives seemed complete. But one day, Martin's wife became ill. Her fever rose day after day. The doctor said there was nothing to be done. She died a week later. Martin felt as though the world had dropped out of his heart. He wept and grieved. Friends comforted him, but he found no release. One day, he looked into the eyes of his little son. He saw his wife's eyes, and there he found hope.

The dragging days of pain became shorter as Martin and the little one played, laughed and walked together. They visited the market. Martin delighted in buying a toy, trinket or an apple for him. The youngster laughed and skipped delightedly beside him. Martin smiled.

A few years passed. One winter the wind was very cold, the sleet and snow bitter. Martin's son started coughing. He looked pale and listless. Martin tried to tempt him with delicacies, little frosted cakes, grapes, anything, but the child wouldn't eat. One morning, Martin found the youngster, still and white, on his bed. Martin wailed. He groaned. He wept. But nothing could bring his son back. Martin's universe collapsed. "It's God's fault," he muttered. He raged at God. "You are unfair," he shouted.

Martin continued to work quietly. He kept to himself. When customers came, he only muttered a few words. He was overcome by grief, anger and great sense of desolation. He no longer went to church.

One day an old peasant-pilgrim, a man of great spiritual depth, visited him. "Martin," he said, "You live for only yourself. You do not trust the great kingdom of God."

"Leave me alone," Martin said, "I have nothing to live for."

"When you live for God, your grief will lessen and your troubles will seem lighter."

"How can I do that?" asked Martin. For a moment his heart throbbed with hope.

"Don't you read?" asked the elder. "Go buy a New Testament and you will find the way."

Martin did. He read the gospel's. Jesus good news brought great comfort to his heart. "Come to me, all you who are burdened..." he read. Day after day he read and meditated on the great teachings of Jesus. He read about Jesus' visit to the home of Simon the Pharisee and thought, "Ah, how splendid it must be to have the Little Father enter one's simple abode."

That night, he heard a voice that wakened him. "Martin, look to the street tomorrow. I am coming to visit you." Martin knew it was the Christ.

Martin got up early, swept the floor, washed the dishes, put on the kettle and watched the window as he worked. No Christ appeared. But he saw an old soldier, weakened by age and service, walking by with a shovel.

"He is so frail," Martin said. "He shouldn't shovel snow in the cold." He ran out and called, "Good man, come in for tea." Stephen gladly accepted.

Martin told him of his vision. "I am waiting for the Christ," he said. And he began to talk to the old man of the Little Father, (his name for Jesus). Tears rolled down the old man's cheeks as he left. He felt a hope in his heart that had long been lost.

Martin waited. It was late afternoon. No Christ appeared. A woman dressed in ragged summer clothes, hugging a baby tightly against her breast, stopped and turned her back to the wind.

"The poor thing," Martin thought. He ran out and brought her in. He gave her soup to eat and held the little one. How like the one he had lost. "I am a soldier's wife but my husband is stationed far away, and I have no money. I had to sell my shawl to buy food."

Martin rummaged in the cupboard and found an old coat. He gave it to her and some money. "Bless you," she whispered, as she walked up the stairs. She turned at the door. "Bless you," she said again.

The sun set. Dusk stole in. No Christ. Martin looked out sadly. He saw an old woman carrying a sack of shavings and a basket with a few apples. She rested by his window and set both sack and basket down. A ragged boy ran up, snatched an apple and scurried away. The old one turned quickly and grabbed him. The boy screamed and flayed about. Martin ran out. "He should be flogged," she cried. Martin talked quietly with them. "The way of Jesus is to forgive," he said.

The baffled boy apologized to the old one. He had fully expected a beating. Martin gave him an apple and paid the woman. "That's how God forgives us," he said. The amazed woman, found comfort in these words. The lad, shook his head. He couldn't believe what was happening. This was so unlike his life on the streets. "Old woman," he said, "I will carry your heavy sack." Together they trudged off.

It was dark now. Martin lit the lamp and put wood on the fire. He heated the soup. Then in a shadowy corner, he saw figures, the old man, the young mother, the old woman and the boy. He heard a whisper in his ear, "Martin, Martin, don't you know me?

"Who are you?" Martin called. Each dusky figure stepped from the corner and said, "It is I." They smiled. Martin didn't understand. He put on his spectacles and read the New Testament where it opened, as of itself. He stopped. He read the words again, "As you did it to one of the least of these...you did it to me." Now Martin understood his vision. Christ had indeed visited that day, and he, Martin had taken him in; the man, the mother, the woman and the boy. And Martin was glad.

Retold and adapted from Leo Tolstoy, Where Love Is, There God Is Also.

I HAVE DECIDED

Anne N, Rupp   Anne N. Rupp

Walking tempo

I have de- cid- ed to fol- low Je-sus,

I have de- cid- ed to fol- low him.

I have de- cid- ed to fol- low Je- sus,

I have de- cid- ed to fol- low him.

Part III

INTERGENERATIONAL WORSHIP AND ACTIVITY

Introduction

The family is a model for intergenerational worship and education. But with today's busy, demanding schedules, it is difficult to retain that concept. Decades ago, when families were larger, sometimes three generations living together, intergenerational learning in the home was assumed; it was a way of living together through sharing, learning and worship. The word 'intergenerational' had not yet been coined as a way of engaging children, youth and adults in the life of the church.

Today's smaller families, and one-parent families, as well as job and career pressures, make it difficult for the family to function as an intergenerational unit. Age categorization keeps generations apart. Children engage in sports and activities planned for them, and parents are involved otherwise. The joint family experience becomes minimal. Some families don't have time to eat together, talk together or share their common lives. Time for worship falls by the wayside. Children are told which chores to do before mother comes home from work, and father drives them to another lesson when he arrives. This spells a great dearth in what has been a strong model for learning and sharing faith with one's children.

The church must take the family model, and provide programs that make it possible for all ages to be family for each other. All ages can nurture and assist each other's spiritual development, through sharing and a common experience. The church needs to provide resources and support to empower families. Families, often far from relatives or childhood friends, can be encouraged to include extended family in their daily lives, as a means of sharing faith and life at all age levels.

The church has much work at hand, if it plans to reinstate the value and importance of the intergenerational learning and worship model. Intergenerational experience is a great leveler. It minimizes the distance between parent-child, or teacher-student. Individuals of all ages grow together in grace and understanding.

Discussing intergenerational worship is one thing. Planning and experiencing it is another. We are accustomed to much talk and discussion in our education programs, particularly in the adult classes. We have lost the ability to play, dramatize and celebrate. That loss may affect how we worship. But Christianity is not a body of knowledge, it is an experience.

Dole's Cone of Learning affirms that we learn the least when being talked to, and the most through direct experience. The closer one comes to the actual experience, the more meaningful it will be. Children are life and experience oriented. We can learn from them. Part III of Walking Towards Pentecost has been planned with shared experience in mind. It provides opportunity for adults, youth and children to participate in mutual growth and worship without feeling that young children need to be talked down to, or that the experience is childish.

It's important for children to learn about the post- Easter events, each one moving through the gospel accounts towards the climax in Acts 2. They are not too young to experience the joy and excitement of the post-resurrection stories leading to Pentecost. By making worship and time together experiential, this joy is caught and shared with all ages. After all, joy is at the heart of the gospel. Joy permeates the lives of young and old as they together live out the collective experience of hope, enthusiasm, and gratitude, engendered by the risen Christ, the magnitude of God, and the Holy Spirit's enpowering force.

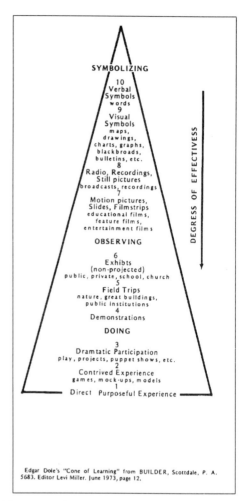

Edgar Dole's "Cone of Learning" from BUILDER, Scottdale, P. A. 5683. Editor Levi Miller. June 1973, page 12.

I. PLANNING AHEAD. Several weeks before Easter an intergenerational group meets to plan the series to come. Each Sunday consists of two parts.

A. __THE__ __WORSHIP__. (20-25 minutes) To assist you in your planning, the topic is followed by an opening section which lists the preparation required in advance. If you follow this closely, the next steps should move smoothly. The worship session begins with a skit. (See Part II Children Worship and Learn for costume ideas.) To make it possible for various ages to participate, without having to improvise, a script has been written for each skit, including actions and stage directions. Try to assign parts to family or extended family units. Rehearsing together at home, enriches their mutual involvement. The theme song, "It's Jesus Christ, Hallelujah!" (Exhibit A-3) is used throughout. Each brief drama is followed by or may incorporate, songs, prayers, and participation at various levels. All ages relive the stories in different ways. The mood throughout is one of joy and celebration.

B. **INTERGENERATIONAL** **ACTIVITIES**. (35-40 minutes) All ages move to the fellowship hall after the worship. Here they choose activities they wish to participate in. Set up tables or areas for each listed activity. To maintain the mood, decorate the tables, hang balloons from the ceiling and posters from the walls. These are the areas available to all ages.

1. __Family__ __Pentecost__ __Wreaths:__ On the first Sunday, families make a wreath with eight candles, one for each Sunday from Easter to Pentecost. Worship booklets for candle lighting services in the home are provided.

Making the Pentecost wreath is a one-Sunday event. On the Sundays that follow, this table will become a <u>Walking Towards Pentecost Activities</u> center. Ideas, patterns and alternatives are provided. You may want to add others.

2. <u>Holy Spirit Banner Center</u>: Determine whether these will be small individual take-home banners or whether many will engage in making one large banner. If you choose the latter, hang it in the sanctuary or fellowship hall on Pentecost morning.

3. <u>Pentecost Tree Decoration Center</u>: The color green, signifies hope. Use green as a symbol of the resurrection hope brought into existence by Easter morning. A tree set up, will be hung with meaningful, theme-related decorations. Directions and patterns are provided.

4. <u>Easter Pentecost Discussion Group:</u> For those less interested in hands-on activities, this group provides opportunity for further discussion of the morning's theme. Group involvement and participation is included.

5. <u>Refreshment Tables</u>: Two options are provided. You may use simple refreshments that grow out of the morning's theme. For example, a suggestion for Travel Food is given on the second Sunday. Or several in the church who like to bake, may want to provide breads and sweets that reflect the Easter-Pentecost season. Some of these recipes come from other countries. Make extra recipe copies, and place on the Refreshment Table, for those interested.

6. <u>The Happy Clown</u> (optional): Each Sunday this figure, representing the resurrected Christ, mixes with and relates to the intergenerational group in theme related ways.

The listed activities will only take place during the first seven Sundays. On the eighth Sunday, Pentecost, all generations celebrate a Pentecost Party in the fellowship hall.

OUTLINE OF EASTER TO PENTECOST INTERGENERATIONAL ACTIVITIES

First Sunday (Easter)

1. Family Pentecost Wreaths and Devotionals.
2. Holy Spirit Banner Center.
3. Pentecost Tree Decoration Center.
4. Easter-Pentecost Discussion Group. (John 20:11-18)
5. Refreshment Tables.
6. The Happy Clown (*optional*)

Second Sunday

1. Walking Towards Pentecost Activities.
2. Holy Spirit Banner Center.
3. Pentecost Tree Decoration Center.
4. Easter-Pentecost Discussion Group. (Luke 24:13-29)

5. Refreshment Tables.

6. The Happy Clown *(optional)*

Third Sunday

1. Walking Towards Pentecost Activities.

2. Holy Spirit Banner Center.

3. Pentecost Tree Decoration Center.

4. Easter-Pentecost Discussion Group. (Luke 24:30-33a)

5. Refreshment Tables.

6. The Happy Clown *(optional)*

Fourth Sunday

1. Walking Towards Pentecost Activities.

2. Holy Spirit Banner Center.

3. Pentecost Tree Decoration Center.

4. Easter-Pentecost Discussion Group.(Luke 24:33b-43)
5. Refreshment Tables.

6. The Happy Clown *(optional)*

Fifth Sunday:

1. Walking Towards Pentecost Activities.

2. Holy Spirit Banner Center.

3. Pentecost Tree Decoration Center.

4. Easter-Pentecost Discussion Group. (John 20:24-31)

5. Refreshment Tables.

6. The Happy Clown *(optional)*

Sixth Sunday

1. Walking Towards Pentecost Activities.

2. Holy Spirit Banner Center.

3. Pentecost Tree Decoration Center.

4. Easter-Pentecost Discussion Group. (John 21:1-17)

5. Refreshment Tables.

6. The Happy Clown *(optional)*

Seventh Sunday (Ascension)

1. Walking Towards Pentecost Activities.
2. Holy Spirit Banner Center.
3. Pentecost Tree Decoration Center.
4. Easter-Pentecost Discussion Group. (Luke 24:50-52, Acts 1:4-11)
5. Refreshment Tables.
6. The Happy Clown *(optional)*

Eighth Sunday (Pentecost):

1. A Pentecost Party.
2. Hanging of the Pentecost Banner.
3. Singing Around the Pentecost Tree.
4. Easter-Pentecost Discussion Group (optional). (Acts 1:12-14, 2:1-14)
5. Pentecost Refreshments.
6. The Happy Clown *(optional)*

"I HAVE SEEN THE LORD!"

John 20:11-18.

GETTING READY: Prepare and do the following in advance:

☐ Ask a youth or adult (who sings well) to take on the role of Mary and learn the song, "Lament," (EXHIBIT A-2) and "It's Jesus Christ, Hallelujah!" (EXHIBIT A-3)

☐ Contact two youth, adults or older children to take on the roles of the two dressed in white.

☐ Solicit a youth or adult to take on the role of Jesus in the skit. If possible, keep this same person and costume throughout the series.

☐ Create a garden scene at the front of your assembly room. If plants are not available, some families and extended families may want to make trees. (*Wrap large cardboard tubes or wooden poles with strips of brown burlap and make puffy, leaf tops from green burlap.*) Others may want to make flowers. (*These may be made from construction paper, colored tissue paper or facial tissue.*) A smaller group may wish to make a tombstone. (*Carve a large piece of styrofoam and spray paint with gray enamel.*)

☐ Plan simple costume for Mary and Jesus.

☐ Make copies of the prayer, *JESUS, FILL OUR HEARTS,* and hand these out as worshipers arrive.

☐ Make a large sign, JERUSALEM, and post where all can see it.

A. THE WORSHIP:

1. Mary, comes down the aisle from back of room, despondently singing "Lament." (EXHIBIT A-2) She stops near the tombstone and faces it in a weeping position. The two in white come in and stand behind the tombstone. Mary bends over and looks at the inscription on the tombstone.

Two in white:	(*in unison*) Why are you crying?
Mary:	My Lord is dead. I weep for my loss. But where is his body? The stone has been rolled away. The tomb is empty. Peter saw it too, and ran to tell the others. (*Pause*) Who has taken away my Lord? Where have they laid him? (*As she speaks, Jesus comes in quietly and stands behind her. The two in white cross their hands over their hearts, look up and remain in this position. Mary turns to search another part of the garden and sees Jesus.*)

Jesus:	Dear woman, why are you crying? Have you lost something? Are you looking for someone? Here in this garden?
Mary:	(*Folds her hands and looks up pleadingly.*) Who are you? Are you the gardener? Have you been here all morning? What happened? Where did they hide my Lord and Master? Tell me and I'll make sure his body is taken to a safe place. (*Jesus doesn't answer*) Please, gardener. Please. (*He still doesn't answer but just looks at her and she turns to continue her search.*)
Jesus:	Mary, oh, Mary!
Mary:	(*She turns, recognizes him and falls on her knees.*) My Lord, my dear teacher, it's you! (*She reaches up to him and stays in this position, eyes closed.*)
Jesus:	Go tell my followers that I am alive... that I am going to the Father, your God and my God.
	(*Jesus and two in white quietly leave and Mary starts singing stanza 1 of "It's Jesus Christ, Hallelujah!"*) (EXHIBIT A-3)

2. Mary slowly rises while singing, faces those gathered for worship and invites them to join her as she sings the stanza again. She steps forward and joyfully sings stanza 2, "I've seen the Lord," (*instead of, "We've"*)

Mary invites all to stand and participate in the unison prayer,

JESUS, FILL OUR HEARTS.

Jesus fill our hearts with music;

Jesus fill our lives with song.

You have made us sons and daughters,

And we praise you all day long.

You are risen Lord, we thank you;

You are with us every day.

Thank you for this Easter morning,

Thank you for this Easter day.

3. Mary concludes the service by asking all to sing an Easter song (*to the tune of Happy Birthday*).

Happy Easter to you. Happy Easter to you.
Happy Easter, dear Jesus. Happy Easter to you.

B. INTERGENERATIONAL ACTIVITIES

Family Pentecost Wreaths and Devotionals.

Follow these steps in advance:

1. Set one or more tables near the main entrance to the fellowship hall. Cover with white paper and add green streamers on the side.

2. Emphasize green as a symbol of hope. Procure artificial greens or twigs from evergreen shrubs or trees. Or pot small philodendrons several months in advance (*one per family unit*), and set these in the middle of the wreath. Loop the vines around the candles.

3. Cut triangles from heavy styrofoam or plywood, measuring 12" on each side. Drill 8 holes for candles, one on each corner, two on either side and 1 in the front middle.

4. Purchase candles, 3 white, 2 pink, 2 rose, and 1 red, for each family unit. Set a poster with instructions and illustrations on the table. Make one wreath in advance, to serve as a model. See illustration below.

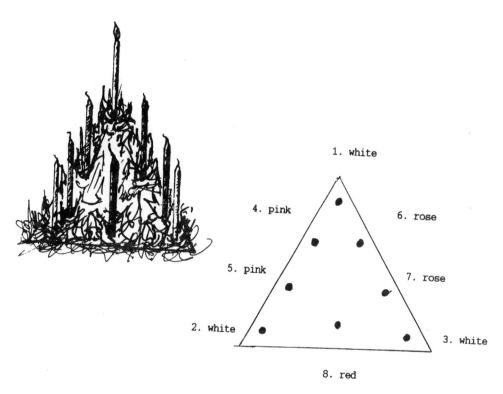

5. Make copies of The Pentecost Wreath (EXHIBIT A-6) and lay on the table or insert in the devotional booklets.

6. Provide a devotional booklet for Easter-Pentecost candlelighting ceremonies in the home.

Option One: If your pastor is not using Part I during this season, use Lighting the Pentecost Wreath in Part I, **THE CONGREGATION AT WORSHIP**, under B. RESOURCES FOR THE SERVICE OF WORSHIP. Cut out the eight services, paste each on a sheet of paper, add visuals and make copies. Design a cover, copy and staple.

Option Two: Use the scripture references listed at the beginning of each session in Part III. Write the reference, then the following: "In the space below, family members may draw a picture about the story. Put yourself in the picture. What do you like about this story? How does it make you feel?"

For each Sunday, read one of the following (listed in consecutive order):

- Think about this story as you light the first white candle on the Pentecost wreath. Remember, Jesus lives. Hallelujah!

- Think about this story as you light the first and second white candles on the Pentecost wreath. Remember, Jesus walks with us, wherever we go.

- Think about this story as you light the three white candles on the Pentecost wreath. Remember, Jesus is with us when we're eating together. Thank him.

- Think about this story as you light the three white candles and one pink one, on the Pentecost wreath. Remember, Jesus fills our life with good surprises.

- Think about this story as you light the three white and two pink candles on the Pentecost wreath. Remember, Jesus is beside us and helps us when bad things happen.

- Think about this story as you light the three white and two pink candles and a rose one on the Pentecost wreath. Remember, Jesus loves us and takes care of us.

- Think about this story as you light the white, pink and rose candles on the Pentecost wreath. Remember to share the good news, "Jesus loves me, Jesus loves you," with others.

- Think about this story as you light all the candles on the wreath, including the red Pentecost candle. Remember the church and the special people in it who show you God's love and care. Say a family prayer of thanks for God, for Jesus, for the Holy Spirit, for family and for the church.

    Option Three: Design your own, using the gifts of all ages in the church. Make it rich with comments, poetry, illustrations and thoughts.

Holy Spirit Banner Center

Make sure to check with your pastor in advance. If your pastor is using materials from Part I, **THE CONGREGATION AT WORSHIP**, he or she may be planning to include the banner making as advised in Part I, First Sunday, under B. RESOURCES FOR WORSHIP, 4. The Pentecost Banner. If so, the intergenerational group may want to make individual banners to take home, or create one banner to hang in the fellowship hall.

In the event that no plans have been made by the pastor, you may agree to hang the banner before or during the worship time. See Part I, Eighth Week, A. THE DRAMA OF WORSHIP, for ways this may be done. If worship precedes church school, you may need to complete the banner a week early, and incorporate week eight with week seven.

Instructions for the Holy Spirit Banner are found in EXHIBIT C-1. Supply cardboard flame patterns of various sizes, scissors, and on this first Sunday provide bright yellow material.

Pentecost Tree Decoration Center

Green can be a symbol of hope during the Easter-Pentecost season, as well as at Christmas. Use an artificial or potted tree. Each Sunday participants make and hang ornaments that reflect the theme of the 50 days from Easter to Pentecost. Set up and decorate a table where the ornaments will be made. Provide tree hooks.

CIRCLES OF THE SON: Resurrection morning is often symbolized by the rising sun and related services because the Son has risen. Give room for creativity. Hang a paper banner above the table with the lettering, WHAT COLOR IS EASTER? Provide pastel markers, chalk or crayons. Cut several 4" cardboard circle patterns. Lay out sheets of white posterboard, pencils, scissors and ornament hooks. Write these instructions on a poster:

CIRCLES OF THE SON

Make an Easter morning sun:

♦ Lay a pattern on posterboard and draw around it.

♦ Cut out the circle and push a hook through it for hanging.

♦ Ask yourself, "What color is Easter?"

♦ Pick a favorite Easter color, one that makes you feel happy.

♦ Color the sun and hang it on the Pentecost tree.

Easter-Pentecost Discussion Group *(Use all or select.)*

Search the Scripture.

❑ Read John 20:1-18

❑ Who are the main characters? Compare this story with other resurrection accounts in Matthew, Mark, Luke.

❑ What is Mary's greatest concern? How is it resolved?

Discuss the Questions.

❑ The joy, excitement and surprise found in the resurrection narratives, are surpassed only by similar emotions in the nativity story (Luke 2:8-20). What is the role of joy in the gospel? How does that joy relate to your own Christian experience? What is the difference between joy and happiness?

Engage in Group Response.

Materials: wire, streamers, ribbons, pipe cleaners, scissors, glue.

❑ Make a stand-up collage to depict your personal understanding of joy. When finished, share with each other.

❑ Prayer of Appreciation: Read Ephesians 1:3 in unison.

Refreshment Table

Cover a table with a bright yellow cloth to match the colors of the flames in the banner. (See Holy Spirit Banner Center.) You have a choice of two types of refreshments, each related to the theme of the morning, or more generally to the Easter-Pentecost season.

EASTER SUN COOKIES.

Buy or make round sugar cookies. Frost with bright yellow frosting.

PASCHA FROM RUSSIA.

Pascha means Easter or Passover, reminiscent of the Pascal lamb, Jesus Christ. This sweet bread is baked and taken to the priest early Easter morning to be blessed, before it is eaten.

- 1 pkg fast rising yeast
- 5 eggs separated
- 1/2 cup sugar
- 1/2 cup melted shortening
- 3 1/2 to 4 1/2 cups flour
- 1/4 cup lukewarm water
- 1 cup lukewarm milk
- rind of 1/2 lemon
- 1 teaspoon salt

Stir 1 teaspoon sugar into water, add yeast and allow to rise 10 minutes. Add shortening, milk, salt and grated lemon rind. In separate bowl, beat egg whites until stiff. Beat egg yolks until lemon colored, add sugar and beat until creamy. Add egg yolks to yeast mixture, then fold in whites.

Add flour, one cup at a time, beating until smooth. Grease hands and knead mixture until smooth, adding the last flour a small amount at a time. Dough should be soft but not sticky. Place in a large greased bowl, brush with oil, cover and let rise in a warm place. After 30 minutes, punch down and let rise again. Form into balls and place in round, greased forms or juice cans. Cover, let rise until double in bulk. Bake at 325 for 45-50 minutes (varies with size of pascha).

When cool, frost, dust with colored sugars, decorate with candy, or sprinkle with silver/gold decors.

The Happy Clown *(optional)*

Jesus is present, dressed as a happy clown, representing the theme each Sunday. On this First Sunday, the clown walks around, mixes with the groups and joyfully hands out flowers to all ages.

"STAY WITH US!"

Luke 24:13-29, Mark 16:12

GETTING READY: Prepare and do the following in advance:

❑ Check to make sure the youth or adult taking on the Jesus role last week is available and maintains the same dress.

❑ Solicit an adult and a youth to take on the roles of Cleopas and friend, in simple costume.

❑ Ask families or children to act as travelers on the road between Jerusalem and Emmaus.

❑ Ask the person who was Mary last Sunday, to return (in costume) as worship and song leader, after the skit.

❑ Make copies of the song, "Praise God," (EXHIBIT A-5) Pass these out as worshipers arrive.

❑ Make a large sign that reads EMMAUS and post it where all can see it.

A. THE WORSHIP:

1. Cleopas and friend walk down the aisle, talking as they walk. Occasionally, other travelers (*individuals or families with children*) meet or pass them and greetings of 'Shalom,' are exchanged.

Cleopas:	It's hard to believe. A little over a week ago, Jesus was riding into Jerusalem on a donkey and the crowds were cheering. Remember how excited they were? (*Travelers pass them.*)
Travelers:	Shalom!
Cleopas & friend:	Shalom! (*Travelers continue down aisle and exit right.*)
Friend:	Yes, we were all excited. Remember how we threw branches on the road as he approached? Some even threw down their robes and shawls. It was like heralding a king.
Cleopas:	As he rode through our midst and the crowd became louder and louder, cheering and shouting, I was sure this was the one we had been waiting for.

Friend:	I can hear them yet: (*They stop, look at each other, then look up, their faces aglow with memory. They raise their arms.*)
Cleopas & friend:	(*unison*) "Hosanna to the Son of David! Blessed is he who comes in the name of the Lord! Hosanna in the highest! (*They turn to the worshipers on either side and encourage them to shout, "Hosanna in the highest," with them as they repeat it several times.*)
Cleopas:	That was quite a day! (*Continue walking. A traveler meets them.*)
Cleopas:	Shalom, my friend.
Traveler:	Shalom. (*They resume their conversation.*)
Friend:	But Jesus always managed to annoy the priests and scribes... remember how he went to the temple right after that grand entrance and chased out the money changers? They didn't like that!
Cleopas:	And then he started healing the blind and the lame, right there in the temple. He wasn't afraid of what the religious leaders thought or what they said. He wasn't scared of criticism.
Friend:	What I remember is the children—you were outside, but crowds of them came right into the temple and started shouting, "Hosanna to the Son of David." Children doing this? Unheard of! (*Jesus comes slowly from behind.*)
Cleopas:	That upset the chief priest and his followers. I guess that's when they really started plotting against him. (*Sighs*) Now it's all over. Our leader is dead! What are we supposed to do now? (*Stop and look at each other. Jesus moves beside them.*)
Jesus:	Shalom, my friends. Where are you going?
Friend:	Shalom. We're going to Emmaus, it's only a few miles from here.
Jesus:	May I join you? What are you talking about?
Cleopas:	We don't know you, but you are welcome to join us. We are talking about what happened in Jerusalem a few days ago. We just came from there.
Jesus:	What do you mean? What things happened? (*A family moves towards them.*)
Family:	(*in unison*) Shalom!
All three:	(*unison*) Shalom! (*Jesus stops, lays his hand on a child's head.*)
Jesus:	Shalom, my little one. (*Child looks at him and smiles. Jesus turns back to Cleopas.*) Now, what were you saying? What has happened?
Cleopas:	Are you the only visitor in Jerusalem who doesn't know about this?
Friend:	Jesus of Nazareth, a mighty prophet of God, who we thought would be the one to redeem Israel.... (*Cleopas interrupts hurriedly.*)

Cleopas:	Yes, indeed, that's what we thought. But the religious leaders didn't like him. They ordered his arrest and managed to have him crucified.
Friend:	Now we don't know what to do. It's three days after his death. Some women got all excited this morning. They came running with a story about the tomb being empty. "Two angels told us Jesus is alive," they said.
Cleopas:	Some of the disciples went back to check things out but they only found an empty tomb. Certainly no Jesus. Somebody stole his body. I'm sure! (*All three reach the front of the room and turn facing the worshipers.*)
Jesus:	Reads Luke 24:25-27 (*The two stare at him, looking puzzled and amazed*)
Cleopas:	The way you talk, makes me feel hopeful again. As if something exciting is going to happen. Maybe he'll be back. (*Jesus smiles*)
Friend:	I want to hear more. It's almost evening and these few miles while you talked, have sped by. See this house? (*Points to an area beside the EMMAUS sign*) This is where we live. Come and stay with us. Please, and then.... (*Cleopas interrupts eagerly.*)
Cleopas:	Then you can tell us more, while we eat together....
Jesus:	(*Looks at them, pauses and nods.*) I will be glad to stay with you, my friends. (*All exit down side aisle. Mary enters down center aisle and reaches the front as the three exit.*)

2. Mary asks, "Who was this stranger?" Gets response from the worshipers. Asks them to join her in singing, stanza 1-2 of, "It' Jesus Christ, Hallelujah!" (EXHIBIT A-3) (*She recites each stanza before singing.*)

Mary says, "We know this stranger was Jesus, so we can worship and celebrate. She leads a unison reading of, "Praise God." (EXHIBIT A-5)

3.Mary concludes the service by asking all to sing a Hosanna song to the tune of Happy Birthday.

> *Hosanna to you! Hosanna to you!*
> *Hosanna in the highest! Hosanna to you!*

B. INTERGENERATIONAL ACTIVITIES

Walking Towards Pentecost Activities

Participants in this center make or engage in one of these activities.

Emmaus Comic Strip.

❏ Lay a simple-to-read version (or a story from a Bible story book) of Luke 24:13-29 on the table. Enlarge the comic strip (on the next page), depicting scenes from the story. Make a number of copies.

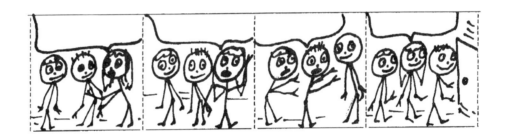

❑ Write these instructions on a stand-up poster and set on the table.

EMMAUS COMIC STRIP

◆ Read the story in (indicate where).

◆ Study the cartoon figures.

◆ Fill in the balloons with your own words.

Jesus Lives Calendar Mobile.

❑ Lay wire coat hangers, construction paper, marking pens, darning needle, yarn, ruler and several 2" cardboard, circle patterns on the table. Enlarge the smile faces below.

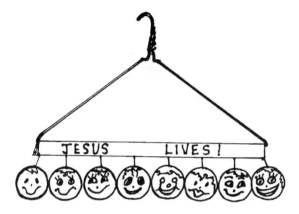

❑ Write these instructions on a poster and set on the table.

JESUS LIVES CALENDAR MOBILE.
Make a mobile.

♦ Fold a sheet of construction paper in half, lengthwise. Cut at the fold. Fold one sheet in half.

♦ Write, JESUS LIVES on the folded sheet and fit over the hanger.

♦ On yellow construction paper, draw around the circle pattern.

♦ Make 8 circles (eight Sundays from Easter to Pentecost).

♦ Draw smile faces on each circle, using ideas from the illustration.

♦ Cut yarn into eight 12-inch lengths. Thread needle with yarn, push through the smile face and tie to the hanger.

♦ At home, color two of the smile faces red. Each Sunday after this, color another smile face. On Pentecost Sunday (eight weeks) your calendar mobile will be finished.

Holy Spirit Banner Center

Instructions for the Holy Spirit Banner are found in Exhibit C-1. Supply cardboard flame patterns of various sizes, scissors, and on this second Sunday provide a striped <u>blue</u> material.

Pentecost Tree Decoration Center

❑ Each Sunday participants make and hang ornaments that reflect the theme of the 50 days from Easter to Pentecost.

❑ **OPEN DOORS**: A symbol for this story is best depicted by an open door to represent hospitality. Cut out the patterns below.

fold back

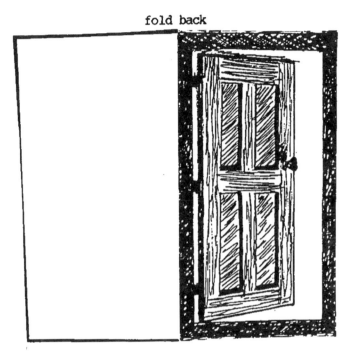

❑ Make copies. Lay these copies, cardboard, glue, scissors and crayons on the table. Write these instructions on a poster.

OPEN DOORS

◆ The open door reminds us that the two from Emmaus invited Jesus to stay with them.

◆ Cut out a door and color it.

◆ Glue the door to cardboard and cut out again.

◆ Hang it on the Pentecost tree.

111

Easter-Pentecost Discussion Group (*Use all or select.*)

Search the Scripture.

❑ Read Luke 24:13-29

❑ List the concerns expressed by the Emmaus disciples. Jesus' response? What is the general mood of this passage?

Discuss the Questions.

❑ What are some ways you help a friend who is depressed, feeling disappointed or experiencing grief? How do you express compassion?

❑ At what point does hope enter the dialogue between Jesus and the two disciples (*compare 24:32*)? How important is hope to your life?

❑ Hospitality to a stranger is a biblical injunction. Compare what happens in this story to Hebrews 13:2. How was hospitality practiced in the home where you grew up?

Engage in Group Response.

Materials: newsprint, marking pen.

❑ Reflect on your hospitality practices. Think of one word to describe them. Print this word on the newsprint. As you write beside or over each other's words, you create a Hospitality Collage.

❑ Talk about what, if anything, you would like to change about your word. Share ways you would like to practice hospitality to a 'stranger' during the Easter-Pentecost season.

Refreshment Table

Cover a table with a striped blue cloth to match the colors of the flames in the banner. (See Holy Spirit Banner Center.) You have a choice of two types of refreshments, each related to the theme of the morning or more generally with the Easter-Pentecost season.

EMMAUS TRAVEL FOOD.

Mix raisins, large crunchy cereal, butterscotch morsels, chocolate chips and miniature marshmallows. Fill 3 ounce paper cups.

HOT CROSS BUNS FROM ENGLAND.

As the Emmaus disciples, reflect sadly on the crucifixion events, it appears timely to eat these buns associated with Good Friday.

- *1 pkg fast rising yeast*
- *3/4 cup lukewarm milk*
- *1/4 cup melted vegetable oil*
- *1/4 cup sugar*
- *1/2 tsp cinnamon*
- *1/4 tsp allspice*
- *1/2 cup lukewarm water*
- *2 eggs*
- *1 tsp salt*
- *2/3 cup currants*
- *1/4 tsp nutmeg*
- *3 1/2 to 4 cups flour*

Stir 1 tsp sugar into warm water and add yeast. Let rise 10 minutes. Beat the eggs and sugar. Add oil, milk, salt and spices. Beat well. Slowly add flour, beating after each addition. Before the last cup, add the currants. Then slowly add flour, and knead until smooth and elastic. Place in a greased bowl, cover and let rise in a warm place. After 15 minutes, knead it again. Do this two more times. Form in about 2 dozen buns and flatten. Brush top with a beaten egg yolk. Let rise until double in bulk. With scissors, snip a cross on the top. Bake at 375 about 25 minutes. While still hot, brush with a glaze of powdered sugar, grated orange peel and milk. When cool, add more powdered sugar to the glaze and form crosses on the buns.

The Happy Clown (*optional*)

Jesus is present, dressed as a happy clown, representing the theme each Sunday. On this Second Sunday, the clown walks around, comforts, listens to and pats shoulders of all ages.

"IT'S HIM!"

Luke 24:30-33a   Mark 16:12

GETTING READY: Prepare and do the following in advance:

- Check to make sure the youth or adult taking on the Jesus role last week is available.

- Draw nail marks on Jesus feet with dark markers.

- Ask the two who took on the roles of Cleopas and friend last week, to do so again.

- Contact some older children, a younger boy and a woman to take on the role of Cleopas' family.

- Provide a basin with water and a towel.

- Set up a table and chairs; place a lit candle in the center.

- Hide a loaf of bread on a platter nearby.

- If you didn't collect copies of the song, "Praise God," (EXHIBIT A-5) after the worship last Sunday, make some additional copies or write the words on a sheet of newsprint. Pass these out as worshipers arrive.

- Make a large sign, EMMAUS, and post where all can see it.

A. THE WORSHIP

1. Rachel, wife of Cleopas, children and grandchild are seated around the table.

Peter:	It's getting late. Where is grandfather?
Rachel:	He went to Jerusalem. He should back soon.
Esther:	Father told me it takes about an hour to walk from Jerusalem to Emmaus. (*Sighs.*) It seems like a long hour.
James:	He must have left very late. I'm getting tired and sleepy.
Peter:	But I don't want to go to bed before I say good-night to grandfather.
Rachel:	Why don't we sing some songs? That will make the time go faster?

(She invites the worshipers to join her. They sing several familiar songs such as, "They Will Know We Are Christians By Our Love," and Jesus Loves Me." During the last stanza, Cleopas, friend and Jesus walk in. Cleopas simulates opening the door.)

Cleopas: Well, here we are. It sounds as if the family is still awake. Come in. We are honored to have you as our guest. *(All three enter.)*

Jesus: Shalom.

Family: Shalom. *(Cleopas directs Jesus to a seat.)*

Cleopas: We have no servants, but as is custom, I will wash your feet. The road from Jerusalem to Emmaus is long and dusty. *(Turns to his daughter.)* Esther, please bring the towel and basin. *(Daughter brings in the basin. He sets it down, removes Jesus' sandals. Cleopas' friend peers over his shoulder.)*

Friend: You have some nasty bruises. Have you been attacked by robbers or a wild beast?

Jesus: No. *(Friend shrugs and sits down. Cleopas washes Jesus' feet.)*
(During the footwashing, Rachel leads the family in singing the following words to the tune of, "It's Jesus Christ, Hallelujah!" EXHIBIT A-3)

Who is this man, Hallelujah? Who is this man, Hallelujah?
Who is this man, who is this man? Who is this man, Amen?

(Rachel beckons the worshipers to join her as they repeat the stanza until Cleopas dries the feet. Cleopas rises and addresses the family.)

Cleopas: This is a friend we met late this afternoon. He has much to say about the Messiah; the one we've been waiting for. We invited him to stay with us.

Rachel: Welcome. I will prepare food. *(She brings in the loaf and sets it on the table. Speaks to Jesus.)* The children and I have eaten earlier. Welcome to our humble home and our simple meal. *(To children)*. Come children, it's time for bed. *(Children get up.)*

Children: Good-night, father.

Peter: Good-night, grandpapa. *(Hugs him.)*

Cleopas: Good night, children. *(They exit. Cleopas motions for Jesus to sit at the head of the table and all take their places.)* May we ask you dear guest, to say the blessing. *(Jesus takes the loaf of bread, holds it and speak the Numbers 6:24-25 benediction blessing:)* The Lord bless you and keep you; the Lord make his face shine upon you and be gracious to you; the Lord turn his face toward you and give you peace. And now, gracious God, come be our guest. And let this food to us be blessed. Amen. *(He breaks the bread and hands a piece to each of them. Cleopas and friend look at each other, shock and surprise registered on their faces. Jesus lays the bread back on the platter and quietly slips out.)*

Friend: *(Whispers.)* It's him. You saw how he broke the bread?

Cleopas:	And that blessing. That familiar blessing. (*Nods*) Yes, it's him. (*Both get up.*)
Cleopas & friend:	It's him. (*They turn and cry out.*) Jesus! (*They look around bewildered.*)
Friend:	He's gone. But he was here. You saw him, didn't you?
Cleopas:	Oh, yes, friend. I did. We've seen the Lord.
Cleopas & friend.	(*Turn to worshipers and say loudly and emphatically.*) We have seen the Lord! (*They lead out in singing stanzas 1-2 of "It's Jesus Christ, Hallelujah!" (EXHIBIT A-3). They motion for worshipers to join them as they repeat the stanzas.*)

2. Friend steps forward and invites worshipers to read, "Praise God," (EXHIBIT A-5) in unison.

3. Cleopas joins his friend and they continue the following dialogue.

Cleopas:	(*Calls.*) Rachel, come here. Please, come here. (*She hurries in.*)
Rachel:	What's wrong?
Cleopas:	Nothing's wrong. Everything's right. That man who was here? That was no ordinary man. That was the Lord.
Friend:	Believe him, Rachel. Believe us both. We have seen the Lord! (*She shakes her head in disbelief but doesn't say anything.*)
Cleopas:	We must hurry back to Jerusalem and tell the disciples. Now.
Rachel:	But it's late! (*Cleopas moves towards her and places his hand on her shoulder.*)
Cleopas:	Late. Early. It doesn't matter. We have good news to tell. Cleopas and friend start singing stanza 3 of "It's Jesus Christ, Hallelujah!" (EXHIBIT A-3) and motion worshipers to sing with them. They move down the aisle singing the stanza several times.

4. Rachel steps forward and leads the worshipers in this short prayer: "Jesus lives. Thank you. Jesus was here. Thank you. We've seen the Lord. Thank you. Amen." She concludes the service by asking all to sing these words to the tune of Happy Birthday.

We're glad you are here. We're glad you are here.
We're glad you're here, Jesus. We're so glad you are here.

B. INTERGENERATIONAL ACTIVITIES

Walking Towards Pentecost Activities

Participants in this center make or engage in one of these activities.

Disciple Word Scramble.

The scrambled letters below, when rearranged, will read, IT IS TRUE! THE LORD HAS RISEN. Enlarge the scramble below and make copies. Lay the copies and pencils on the table.

DISCIPLE WORD SCRAMBLE (Luke 24:33-35)

The letters below are mixed up. If you arrange them in the right order, they will make a seven word sentence. Write each letter you use into the blank spaces. You may only use a letter once.

R H S A U I

E S N O S D

T E L R I R

"IT __ ____! THE ____ ___ _____."

Emmaus Disciple Bread.

Buy several cans of biscuits or crescent rolls from your grocer's dairy case. Meet in the church kitchen with this group. Follow instructions and bake. While you bake, note how Jesus broke bread with the Emmaus disciples, late in the evening, on Easter Sunday. Bread reminds us of Jesus love for us. Once baked, they sample some. Instruct them to walk around, offering, EMMAUS DISCIPLE BREAD to all ages.

Holy Spirit Banner Center

❑ Instructions for the Holy Spirit Banner are found in Exhibit C-1. Supply cardboard flame patterns of various sizes, scissors, and on this third Sunday provide a dotted <u>green</u> material.

Pentecost Tree Decoration Center

❑ Each Sunday participants make and hang ornaments that reflect the theme of the 50 days from Easter to Pentecost.

❑ **SHARED BREAD**: A symbol for this story is best depicted by bread or rolls to represent communion with Christ through the bread broken.

❑ Lay magazines, scissors, glue, posterboard on the table. Write these instructions on a poster.

```
┌─────────────────────────────────────────────┐
│                                             │
│             SHARED BREAD                    │
│                                             │
│       Bread reminds us of Jesus, who broke  │
│    bread, and the Emmaus disciples recognized him. │
│                                             │
│    ◆ Cut pictures of bread or rolls from a  │
│      magazine.                              │
│                                             │
│    ◆ Glue the bread onto the poster board and │
│      cut out again.                         │
│                                             │
│    ◆ Hang it on the Pentecost tree.         │
│                                             │
│    ◆ Optional: Hang different sizes of pretzels │
│      on the tree.                           │
│                                             │
└─────────────────────────────────────────────┘
```

Easter-Pentecost Discussion Group *(Use all or select)*

Search the Scripture.

☐ Read Luke 24:30-33a

☐ List the steps that led to the recognition of Jesus.

☐ What does Luke mean by, "their eyes were opened." Why did they not recognize Jesus earlier? What is the significance of the broken bread?

☐ It was night, Jerusalem lay 7 miles distant, yet the two hurried back to the city. List 7 verbs to describe verses 30-33a.

Discuss the Questions.

☐ Surprise and joy, brought about by a sudden recognition of Christ, are the key elements of this story. Talk about times you have experienced the presence of Christ. How did you recognize that presence? Was surprise involved?

☐ How is your faith affected by the knowledge that Christ's presence is to be assumed, but recognition of that presence depends on us? What kind of signs or symbols do we need, to remind us of Matthew 28:20b?

☐ Share a time when "your eyes were opened." What does that statement mean to you?

Engage in Group Response.

Materials: pencils, paper.

☐ Write a prayer of thanksgiving for specific times you recognized Christ's presence.

☐ Take turns reading your prayers. When all are finished, close with a unison, Amen.

Refreshment Table

Cover a table with a dotted green to match the colors of the flames in the banner. (See Holy Spirit Banner Center.) You have a choice of two types of refreshments, each related to the theme of the morning or more generally with the Easter-Pentecost season.

Raisin Bread.

Buy raisin bread and slice it as participants arrive. Sprinkle each slice with cinnamon sugar, and hand individual slices to all ages coming to the table.

Easter Cookies From Greece.

- *1/2 cup sugar*
- *1/2 tsp salt*
- *1/2 tsp maple flavoring*
- *1 tsp baking powder*
- *2 to 2 1/4 cups flour*

- *1 cup margarine*
- *3 egg yolks*
- *1 tsp vanilla*
- *1/2 tsp cream of tartar*
- *3/4 tsp clove*

Cream sugar and margarine. Add eggs, salt and flavorings. Beat well. Sift flour with baking powder, cream of tartar and cloves. Stir into egg mixture and blend well. Cool for several hours. Shape into small balls and bake 10-12 minutes at 350. Dust with powdered sugar.

The Happy Clown *(optional)*

Jesus is present, dressed as a happy clown, representing the theme each Sunday. On this Third Sunday, the clown walks around, mixes with the groups, and joyfully hands out extra refreshments.

"WE'VE SEEN THE LORD!"

Luke 24:33b-43 John 20:19-21

GETTING READY: Prepare and do the following in advance:

❑ Check to make sure the youth or adult taking on the Jesus role earlier is available.

❑ Draw nail marks on Jesus' hands and feet with dark markers.

❑ Ask the adult and youth who took on the roles of Cleopas and friend earlier, to do so again.

❑ Solicit an individual to take on the role of Simon Peter. (If possible, keep this same person throughout the remaining sessions.)

❑ Contact a number of adults and youth to take on the roles of the eleven and some additional followers.

❑ Set up a small table with a dish of food on it and a lit candle.

❑ Lay a Bible, open at Luke 24 on the table.

❑ Set benches or chairs in a U shape to provide seating for all.

❑ Get or make a large key.

❑ If you didn't collect copies of the song, "Praise God," (EXHIBIT A-5) after the worship last Sunday, make some additional copies (or write the words on a sheet of newsprint). Pass these out as worshipers arrive.

❑ Post the sign, JERUSALEM.

A. THE WORSHIP

1. A disciple enters stealthily from left side, simulates opening and closing a door, and sits down at the table. He looks around fearfully, shades the candle with his hand as though trying to block the light. Others come in, opening and closing the door behind them. Their furtive glances show their fear. They talk in low voices and sit down.

John:	We don't know what's happening in the city center. We're probably all suspect, so we must be careful.
Nathanael:	They got him and now they're sure to go after us.

Sarah:	What about the rumors that came from the Marys and Joanna?
Hannah:	You mean their stories about the angels? Angels who told them Jesus was alive? I don't believe it!
James:	This ordeal has been too much for my mother. I've urged her to get some rest. (*Andrew comes in.*)
Andrew:	Has anyone seen Peter? He told me this morning, that the tomb was empty. What's going on?
Bartholomew:	Probably one of Caiaphas' tricks. Let's keep away. It may be a trap. (*Peter runs down the side aisle and barges in. He is panting.*)
Peter:	You won't believe this. I have seen the Lord! Just a short distance from here. I saw him. I know it was him. He spoke to me. (*All jump up, talking excitedly as they gather around Peter.*)
Nathanael:	I'm going to lock the door. (*Goes to door with the key and locks it.*) There's something strange going on. I don't like this. It could be another trick.
John:	But if it's true? (*Cleopas and friend hurry down side aisle.*) Oh, friends, if it's true? (*There's loud pounding on the door. They all back up and look fearfully towards the door.*)
Bartholomew:	Soldiers. I know it's soldiers.
Cleopas & friend:	Let us in. It's us. Let us in. (*Nathaniel goes to the door and unlocks it. The two stumble in. He locks the door behind them.*)
Nathaniel:	Shalom. What are you doing here this late at night. I thought you went back to Emmaus.
Cleopas:	(*Talks fast and excitedly.*) We have seen the Lord. We have seen the Lord. (*As they talk, Jesus comes down the center aisle.*)
Friend:	We were on our way to Emmaus and this stranger joined us. He was different. He started telling us about the Christ. The more he talked, the more my heart burned with hope and joy.
Cleopas:	We invited him to stay with us but we didn't know it was him.
Friend & Cleopas:	But then he blessed the bread and broke it.
Cleopas:	Our eyes were opened, we both recognized him at the same time. But when we looked up, he was gone.
Bartholomew:	Incredible.
Hannah:	Unbelievable. Come sit down, you must be tired. (*Jesus moves into their midst but no one notices.*)
Jesus:	Shalom. Peace be with you. (*They all back away, hands up or arms shielding their eyes.*)
Matthew:	This makes no sense.
Philip:	It's a ghost. (*All start to murmur the words over and over again. Jesus moves in closer.*)

121

Jesus:	Friends, I am not a ghost. Look at the marks on my hands and feet. Come here touch me. Don't be afraid. It's me. Ghosts don't have bones and warm skin, do they? (*John comes closer, grasps Jesus' hands and falls on his knees.*)
John:	O beloved, master. Is it really you? (*All except Peter crowd around Jesus, expressing amazement and joy. They fall on their knees in worship. They speak words like, "It's Jesus!" "Glory to God," or, "Master, master." Jesus glances over their heads at Peter.*)
Jesus:	Have you anything to eat? (*Peter looks relieved and happy that Jesus recognizes him. He responds eagerly.*)
Peter:	Fish. We have fish. (*He hurries to the table, picks up the dish and brings it to Jesus.*)

2. While Jesus eats, Peter and disciples lead out and motion the worshipers to join them in singing stanza 1-2 of "It's Jesus Christ, Hallelujah!" (EXHIBIT A-3). Jesus moves to table and picks up the Bible.

Jesus:	Listen brothers and sisters. (*He reads Luke 24: 44-49. All get up, face the worshipers and motion them to join in singing stanza 4 of "It's Jesus Christ, Hallelujah!" [EXHIBIT A-3]. Jesus walks out down center aisle followed by all except Peter.*)

3. Peter quotes or reads Job 19:25 with great conviction and joy. He asks worshipers to stand and join in unison reading of the song, "Praise God," (EXHIBIT A-5). He leads the worshipers in this short prayer: "Jesus lives. Thank you. Jesus was here. Thank you. We have seen the Lord. Thank you. Amen." He concludes the service by asking all to sing these words to the tune of Happy Birthday.

> We're happy it's you. We're happy it's you.
> We're happy dear Jesus. We're so happy it's you.

B. INTERGENERATIONAL ACTIVITIES

Walking Towards Pentecost Activities

Participants in this center make or engage in one of these activities.

FRIENDLY GHOST.

☐ The disciples thought they saw a ghost when Jesus appeared (Luke 24:37). Lay white tissue, cotton balls, thin ribbon and fine pointed marking pens on the table. Also open an easy-to-read version of Luke, or a Bible story book, and lay beside the pens. Write these instructions on a stand-up poster and set on the table.

<table>
<tr><td align="center">FRIENDLY GHOST</td></tr>
<tr><td>◆ Read the story in (indicate where).</td></tr>
<tr><td>◆ Place a cotton ball in the center of a tissue.</td></tr>
<tr><td>◆ Pull the tissue tightly under the ball and tie with ribbon.</td></tr>
<tr><td>◆ Draw a friendly face on the ghost.</td></tr>
<tr><td>◆ QUESTION: Who was the 'ghost' in the story?</td></tr>
</table>

HAPPY BANNER.

Two words that describe the disciples reaction when they recognized Jesus are JOY and AMAZEMENT (John 20:20 says, OVERJOYED).

❑ Cut red burlap or heavy cotton into strips, 2'x1'. Fold back 1" at the top and sew a seam. Cut thin dowels into 14" lengths. Lay the strips, some felt squares, cord, balls of yarn, large lettering guides, pens, sharp pencils, size 00 crochet hooks, glue, dowels and scissors on the table. Make copies of the fringe instructions below and lay on the table. Learn how to make a simple fringe and use it as a model at the center.

❑ Place illustration and model on table. Be available to instruct and assist participants.

❑ Write these instructions on a stand-up poster.

HAPPY BANNER

Make a happy banner for your room.

◆ Think of words that mean 'joy.'

◆ Use the lettering guides (or use your own letters) to make the words.

◆ Glue your words onto the banner, in any way you wish.

◆ Push the dowel through the top opening.

◆ Cut a 2-foot cord and tie onto each end of the dowel.

◆ Make yarn fringes for the bottom. (*See instructions*)

Holy Spirit Banner Center

Instructions for the Holy Spirit Banner are found in Exhibit C-1. Supply cardboard flame patterns of various sizes, scissors, and on this fourth Sunday provide a <u>pink</u> material.

Pentecost Tree Decoration Center

❑ Each Sunday participants make and hang ornaments that reflect the theme of the 50 days from Easter to Pentecost.

❑ **FISH AND TOOTHPICKS**: A symbol for this story may be that of fish, which Jesus ate to prove his resurrection (Luke 24:40-43). Provide toothpicks, wood glue, tissue paper, construction paper, fine-lined marking pens, and fish patterns. Lay them on the table. *(Colored toothpicks can be made by dipping into food coloring.)* Make a model in advance to show. Be available to help them with making these polygon-shaped ornaments.

❑ Write these instructions on a poster.

FISH AND TOOTHPICKS

◆ Fish remind us of what Jesus ate to prove he was real.

◆ Lay 5 toothpicks into a five-sided shape.

◆ Glue the toothpicks together at the corners.

◆ Add and glue two more layers (total 15 toothpicks).

◆ Cut a 6-inch square of tissue paper.

◆ Draw around the fish pattern on construction paper.

◆ Cut out the fish and glue onto the center of the tissue.

◆ With pens, put markings on the fish.

◆ Glue the toothpick frame onto the tissue paper.

◆ When dry, hang it on the Pentecost tree.

Easter-Pentecost Discussion Group *(Use all or select)*

Search the Scripture.

❏ Read Luke 24: 33b-43

❏ List the stages of self-revelation by Christ in this story. What did it take to convince the disciples that Jesus lives?

❏ List the responses of the disciples. Compare with John 20:19-23.

Discuss the Questions.

❏ The disciples needed much evidence before they could believe. How is that different or similar to the way you respond to Christ?

❏ How often have you prayed for relief, but when it came, you found yourself attributing the help to luck or chance? Talk about why it is hard to believe in the intangible, let alone the tangible.

Engage in Group Response.

Materials: pencils, paper.

❏ Write your own Confession of Faith, not in terms of doctrine but from personal experience. Make your statement and follow it with a personal life event to verify it. For example: "I believe God answers prayer. On July 13 I...." List as many beliefs and verifications possible, within the given time. Share with each other. Bow in silent prayer.

Refreshment Table

Cover a table with a pink cloth to match the colors of the flames in the banner. See 2. Holy Spirit Banner Center.) You have a choice of two types of refreshments, each related to the theme of the morning or more generally with the Easter-Pentecost season.

Hope And Joy Marshmallows.

- *2 cups sugar*
- *2 envelopes gelatin*
- *1 egg white*

- *1 cup water*
- *6 tablespoons cold water*
- *1 tsp vanilla*

Dissolve gelatin in the cold water. Boil sugar and cup of water for 5 minutes. Remove, add gelatin mixture and stiffly beaten egg white. Beat until the mixture forms stiff peaks. Pour into 6"x10" greased pan. Cool. Dip a sharp knife into cold water, and cut into 40 squares.

Color red and green flaked coconut with food coloring, to symbolize hope and joy. Roll the marshmallow squares in red or green coconut.

Festival Bread From Mexico

- *2 pkg fast rising yeast*
- *1 tsp vanilla*
- *1 cup lukewarm milk*
- *1/3 cup oil*
- *1 whole egg*
- *4 to 5 cups flour*

- *1/2 cup lukewarm water*
- *1 tsp salt*
- *1 tsp grated lemon peel*
- *3 egg yolks*
- *1/2 cup raisins*

Stir 1 tsp sugar into warm water and add yeast. Let rise 10 minutes.

Beat the eggs and sugar until lemon colored. Add oil, milk, salt and vanilla. Add the yeast mixture. Slowly add flour, beating after each addition. Before the last cup, add the raisins. Then slowly add flour, and knead until smooth and elastic. Place in a greased bowl, cover and let rise in a warm place until double in bulk. Knead lightly and cut into eight balls to form small loaves. Shape and place on a greased sheet about 3 inches apart. Flatten to 1/2 inch thick. Make a slash across the loaves with a sharp knife. Let rise until double in bulk. Before baking, brush with beaten egg yolk. Bake at 350 for 20-25 minutes. Decorate with frosting and sprinkle edges with sesame seed. Cut in slices.

Adapted from: Voth, Norma Jost, <u>Festive Breads of Easter</u>. Herald Press, Scottdale, PA, 1980, page 71. Used by permission.

The Happy Clown *(optional)*

Jesus is present, dressed as a happy clown, representing the theme each Sunday. On this Fourth Sunday, the clown walks around, and springs happy surprises on all ages.

"MY LORD AND MY GOD!"

John 20:24-31

GETTING READY: Prepare and do the following in advance:

- ❑ Check to make sure the youth or adult taking on the Jesus role earlier is available.
- ❑ Draw nail marks on Jesus' hands and feet with dark markers.
- ❑ Ask the individual who took on the role of Simon Peter last week, to do so again.
- ❑ Solicit a youth or adult to take on the role of Thomas.
- ❑ Contact some of the adults and youth who participated last week, to again be part of a skit.
- ❑ Set up a small table and several chairs nearby.
- ❑ Have the key used last week, available.
- ❑ Make a sign, ONE WEEK LATER, and use as indicated.
- ❑ Learn the music for the song, "Praise God," (EXHIBIT A-5). (May also be sung to the melody of the doxology, "Praise God from Whom All Blessings Flow.")
- ❑ Make copies of the responsive reading, *NOW I BELIEVE,* and hand these out as worshipers arrive.
- ❑ Retain the sign JERUSALEM, posted as last week.

A. THE WORSHIP

1. Peter and Thomas walk down side aisle and move towards the front. They talk as they walk. John walks slowly down the center aisle. Nathaniel sits near table.

Peter:	Thomas, I've been looking for you. Where were you last night? We were all at John's place. Actually we were all staying together because it's not safe to be out on the street. (*Looks around.*) Even now, we need to be careful.
Thomas:	I think you're making too much of this, Peter. Our leader is dead. The whole thing is going to blow over in no time. Caiaphas will soon forget about us. (*Stops and looks at Peter.*) Where was I last night? Walking. I went back to the Mount of Olives where he spent those last dreadful hours. And I walked by the upper room where we ate the

	Seder—only a few days ago. It never occurred to me that night, that I would never see my master again.
Peter:	(*Urgently.*) But that's what I want to tell you. Remember Easter morning, when the women came running from the tomb? Remember how we shrugged off their stories; ridiculous stories we thought. (*They arrive center front.*)
Thomas:	Just wishful thinking. I don't know what got into them.
Peter:	Well their story is true. I've seen the Lord.
Thomas:	(*Steps back in disbelief.*) What?
Peter:	(*Eagerly.*) Yes, yesterday. And I ran to John's house to tell him. I knew Andrew was there. In fact, everybody was there except you. Thomas, believe me, I've seen the Lord.
Thomas:	(*Puts a consoling hand on Peter's shoulder.*) Peter, these last days have just been too much for you. I know how you must feel. I ran away when they arrested him. Just plain scared. You? You tried to be faithful but you denied him. Your guilt and grief are getting the better of you. You're seeing things.
Peter:	Oh no, Thomas. There's more. Listen to this. Shortly after I arrived at John's, Cleopas and his friend came storming in. They said, Jesus walked with them to Emmaus. He ate supper with them.
Thomas:	(*Sarcastically.*) Why didn't they bring him along to John's house?
Peter:	But that's the good part. (*John walks in.*) Tell him John what happened.
John:	We saw the Lord. All of us. Suddenly he was right there. He showed us his wounds, let us touch him and ate some fish. I can't explain it, but one thing I know. Jesus lives.
Thomas:	(*Shakes his head.*) This is all fine and good for you. But I won't believe unless I see and touch the nail marks in his hands and the wound in his side. (*Miserably.*) I can't believe it, Peter. I just can't believe it, John. (*Thomas exits down center aisle. Peter and John sit down at the table, look at each other and shake their heads. Disciples and other followers come in from all sides and enter through the door. They sing stanzas 1-3 of "It's Jesus Christ, Hallelujah!" (EXHIBIT A-3), and motion the worshipers to join them. They look happy as they move center front and form a semi circle behind Peter and John. Nathanael goes to the door and locks it with the key. A follower holds up the sign, ONE WEEK LATER, for all to see. Disciples and worshipers continue singing, first, "Jesus Loves Me," and then "Praise God," (EXHIBIT A-5). Thomas comes hurriedly down the side aisle and pounds on the door. Nathanael unlocks the door and locks it again after Thomas enters.*)
Thomas:	What is going on here? I heard you half a block away. How can you sing at a time like this? Our beloved master is hardly cold in the grave, the time of mourning has just begun and you're singing like children on a picnic. (*Exasperated.*) How can you be so shallow? (*Jesus moves down side aisle.*)

Nathanael:	Andrew, Peter, shall we tell him?
Peter:	I already tried. He just won't believe it.
Thomas:	Believe what?
All in a Chorus:	That WE HAVE SEEN THE LORD! (*Thomas sits down beside table and waves them away. He looks sad and appears to be crying. Jesus enters.*)
Jesus:	Shalom. Peace with you. (*Surprised disciples and others begin to whisper to each other, louder and louder.*)
All in a Chorus:	It's him. It's him. It's the Lord. (*They come closer.*)
Nathanael:	(*To Peter.*) How did he get in? I locked the door. (*Thomas is watching Jesus and half rises, dumbfounded. Jesus looks at him and moves closer.*)
Jesus:	Thomas? (*Reaches out his hands.*) (*louder*) Thomas?
Thomas:	Y-y-y-yes.
Jesus:	Touch my hands and feel the nail marks. Here, touch my side. The wound has not yet healed. It is I. (*Thomas falls on his knees in worship.*)
Thomas:	My Lord and my God. (*Jesus takes him by the hand and lifts him to his feet.*)
Jesus:	Believe Thomas. Believe. It's hard to believe something if you can't prove it or see it, isn't it? In these days since my resurrection, I have appeared to many, many people. And now to you. It seems that each one, even your friends here (*indicates the disciples*) couldn't believe until they saw me. What a great joy and blessing it is for those who can believe even if they don't see, even if they don't have proof. Never lose faith Thomas. When hard times come. Believe.

2. Jesus exits down center aisle and all except Thomas follow him. Thomas leads them and the worshipers in joyful singing of stanzas 4-5 of, "It's Jesus Christ, Hallelujah!" (EXHIBIT A-3)

3. Thomas says a few words about what this experience means to him and leads the group in the responsive reading, *NOW I BELIEVE.*

Thomas:	Now I believe! Behold I bring you news of great joy Which shall be to all people. Christ is risen indeed!
Response:	Glory to God in the highest And on earth peace. Christ is risen indeed!

4. Thomas concludes the service by asking all to sing these words to the tune of Happy Birthday.

We're happy it's you. We're happy it's you.
We're happy, dear Jesus. We're so happy it's you.

B. INTERGENERATIONAL ACTIVITIES:

Walking Towards Pentecost Activities

Participants in this center make or engage in one of these activities.

Fruit Of The Spirit Mobile.

❑ Provide a large styrofoam circle and twist red ribbon or foil gift wrap around it. Lay cardboard patterns of eight fruits, construction paper, heavy thread, darning needles and a 12-foot cord on the table, for this group project. Write FRUIT OF THE SPIRIT at the top of a sheet of newsprint and print Galatians 5:22-23 on it. Place on nearby wall or easel. Write these instructions on a stand-up poster.

FRUIT OF THE SPIRIT MOBILE

To follow Jesus means we want to live the Jesus way. Paul writes about this, using fruit tree language. Read Galatians 5:22-23.

Plan together as a group:

◆ Each one chooses a fruit of the Spirit.

◆ Choose a fruit pattern and a color of construction paper.

◆ Cut out your fruit, write the Spirit fruit name on it.

◆ Thread the needle, using 24 inches of thread.

◆ Push through your fruit and tie.

◆ Tie the other end to the red circle.

◆ Work together as a group.

◆ Decide how and where you will hang this mobile.

◆ Listen to each other for good ideas.

Cross Bookmark.

❑ The empty cross is a symbol of the resurrection and our faith in a risen Lord. Provide plastic webbing. Cut a strip, 6"x1/2" and another 2 1/2"x 1/2" diagonally for each cross. Study the illustration below and draw or make enlarged copies to lay on the table.

❑ Lay these crosses, yarn and darning needles on the table. Also a bottle of clear nail polish. Partially complete one or more, to serve as a guide for the group. Be sure to cut the webbing diagonally. Note that all stitches are diagonal. Stitch the short piece first and the long one over it, to fasten them to each other, so you have stitched through both strips. Be available at the center to instruct and guide.

❑ Write these instructions on a stand-up poster.

CROSS BOOKMARK

Select a long and short strip for your cross.

◆ Choose a yarn color.

◆ Thread your needle and start at one end of the short piece.

◆ Leave about 1/4 inch yarn at end to be glued down later.

◆ Look closely at the model and make diagonal stitches.

◆ At the middle, make your stitches go the other way.

◆ Follow the same instructions for the long piece.

◆ 2 inches from the top, lay the short piece over it.

◆ Stitch through both pieces to hold them together.

◆ Change direction where the arms of the cross meet.

◆ When finished, cut, dab nail polish to end and hold.

◆ Cut yarn and apply polish to the short piece and hold.

◆ Once the yarn holds, let loose and allow to dry.

Holy Spirit Banner Center

☐ Instructions for the Holy Spirit Banner are found in Exhibit C-1. Supply cardboard flame patterns of various sizes, scissors, and on this fifth Sunday provide a <u>mauve</u> material.

Pentecost Tree Decoration Center

☐ Each Sunday participants make and hang ornaments that reflect the theme of the 50 days from Easter to Pentecost.

☐ **HANDS OF FAITH**: A symbol for this story is best depicted by hands, to represent Jesus proof of faith for Thomas. Lay sheets of black, brown, beige and flesh colored construction paper, scissors and pencils on the table. Write these instructions on a poster.

HANDS OF FAITH

When Jesus showed Thomas his hands, Thomas believed.

◆ Make hands to remind you of Jesus.

◆ Select a sheet of construction paper.

◆ Draw around your hand and cut it out.

◆ Put on special markings from your hand.

◆ Hang it on the Pentecost tree.

Easter-Pentecost Discussion Group *(Use all or select)*

Search the Scripture.

☐ Read John 20:24-31

☐ What proofs did Thomas require before he could believe?

☐ Compare the proofs given in Luke 24:33-43 to those required by Thomas. Why is Thomas singled out as the one with less faith?

☐ Compare the response of the disciples in the Luke story to that of Thomas. What does this say to you?

Discuss the Questions.

☐ It appears that in the Luke narrative, Christ gives evidence in response to fear, but in the Thomas incident he responds to demand of proof. Which of the characters in these stories is most like you? Share and discuss.

☐ Thomas' response is one of worship. Compare with Job's response (Job 42:5). What does worship mean to you? Share a time where you have been overwhelmed and awed by the greatness of God.

Engage in Group Response.

Materials: a worship center with a lit candle, Bibles for all.

❑ Kneel or sit around the worship center and reflect on God's infinite love, compassion and mercy. Group members in turn read these passages in quiet, reflective voices: (*Write these scripture references on slips of paper and give one to each member before the session begins*) Psalm 8:1, 16:7-8, 18:1-2, 19:1-4, 23:1, 33:1-3, 34:1-4, 40:1-3, 47:1-2, 86:1-4, 89:1-2, 90:1-2, 91:1-2, 96:1-4. Close by reading Psalm 100 in unison.

Refreshment Table

Cover a table with a mauve cloth to match the colors of the flames in the banner. (See Holy Spirit Banner Center.) You have a choice of two types of refreshments, each related to the theme of the morning or more generally with the Easter-Pentecost season.

A. **FAITH COOKIES.** Buy or make chocolate cookies or gingersnaps. With a frosting tip, mark a cross on each one.

B. **EASTER BABKA* FROM POLAND.** (*No kneading*)

- 2 pkg fast rising yeast
- 3/4 cup sugar
- 1 cup lukewarm milk
- 1 tsp grated lemon rind
- 1 tsp vanilla
- 2 3/4 to 3 cups flour
- 1/2 cup chopped candied peel
- 1/2 cup lukewarm water
- 15 egg yolks
- 1/2 cup oil
- 1/3 tsp almond extract
- 1 tsp salt
- 1/2 cup chopped, blanched almonds

Stir 1 tsp sugar into warm water and add yeast. Let rise 10 minutes.

Beat the eggs and sugar until lemon colored. Add oil, milk, salt and vanilla, almond extract and lemon rind. Add the yeast mixture. Slowly add flour and beat with mixer for about 10 minutes. Stir in the peel and chopped almonds. Place in a greased bowl, cover and let rise in a warm place until double in bulk. Punch or stir down and let rise again. Grease and flour a 12" fluted pan and fill 1/2 full. Let rise to top of pan and bake at 350 for about 50 minutes. Cool, loosen, and place on a plate. Drizzle with a glaze made of 1 cup powdered sugar, 2 tbsp lemon juice and 1/2 tsp grated lemon rind. *Babka means 'grandmother' or 'woman.' The fluted pan represents her skirt.

Adapted from: Voth, Norma Jost, <u>Festive Breads of Easter.</u> Herald Press, Scottdale, PA, 1980, page 38-40 Used by permission.

The Happy Clown *(optional)*

Jesus is present, dressed as a happy clown, representing the theme each Sunday. On this Fifth Sunday, the clown walks around, mixes with the groups and quietly shows the marks on hands and feet. At closing time, shouts, "Hallelujah, Hallelujah!"

"IT IS THE LORD!"

John 21:1-14

GETTING READY: Prepare and do the following in advance:

- ❑ Check to make sure the youth or adult taking on the Jesus role earlier is available.

- ❑ Contact the persons who took on the roles of Peter, John, James, Thomas, Nathaniel earlier and also two other disciples.

- ❑ Get a cloak for Peter.

- ❑ Fishing rods for the disciples (*or some nets.*)

- ❑ Blue streamers attached on the chairs (*surrounding the worshipers*), about 5' from the back, 3' from the walls on either side and about 10' from the front (*creates an oblong shaped lake*).

- ❑ Make a large sign, SEA OF GALILEE, and place on an easel inside the lake or hang from the ceiling, visible to all.

- ❑ Place the JERUSALEM sign above the door at the rear of the room, where all can see it.

- ❑ Arrange 6 chairs or stools in three rows, in the aisle near front of room (*to represent a boat*).

- ❑ Make a number of large cardboard fish and place in a mesh sack.

- ❑ Make small paper fish for all worshipers and hand these out as they enter.

- ❑ Lay some firewood and a skillet on the shore, at the center.

- ❑ Set a table, back from the firewood and on it have a platter of donuts, some paper cups and pitchers of orange juice (for all worshipers).

- ❑ Write out John 3:16 and post on newsprint where all can see.

- ❑ Ask a quartet or octet to sing, "Holy Spirit, Come with Power" (EXHIBIT C-2) each of the next two Sundays.

A. THE WORSHIP

1. The seven disciples stand at the rear door. They speak in loud voices so all can hear. Peter holds the mesh sack with fish under his cloak.

Peter:	How much longer is this to go on? We've waited and waited here in Jerusalem and nothing has happened. I haven't seen the Lord for weeks. Where is he?

134

John:	I don't know, Peter. But you must not be so impatient. Let's wait a little longer. (*Others murmur to each other.*)
Peter:	Wait? I'm not a waiter, I'm a doer. And besides, I have a family to support. I haven't given them much time these last few years. (*Speaks urgently and increasingly faster.*) My oldest son carried on the fishing business but it's not going too well. And then there's my mother-in-law. I got a message that she's sick again.
Nathanael:	What are you saying? Are you going home? Are you just going to give up and pretend these last three years never happened?
Peter:	No, no, that's not what I'm saying. I'm saying, I'm going back to Galilee. Back to the sea. I'm going out to fish. (*Picks up a rod or net and starts down left aisle.*)
James:	I'll come with you.
Disciples chorus:	We'll all go with you. (*They pick up rods and nets and follow Peter. They enter the boat and sit on the chairs facing the worshipers. As Peter enters the boat, he lays the sack with fish on the floor to the right of the boat, removes his cloak and stands behinds the others.*)
Peter:	Ah! Nothing like the smell of the Sea of Galilee early in the morning. Now let's row out from the shore. The sun is down, soon it'll be dark, and the fish should be biting. (*They row.*)
John:	Looks like a good spot to me. Remember? Three years ago? We fished all night and caught nothing? Then the Lord appeared and told us to go out into the deep water and soon both boats were filled. This is the spot.
James:	Well, he's not here now, so we'll have to fend for ourselves. (*They fish to the left side. While fishing they sing the familiar, "Row, Row, Row Your Boat," several times. Peter, looks over the sea and motions the worshipers to join in.*)
Thomas:	(*Pulls in his line.*) It's no use. We've fished all night. Nothing. We may as well go back. The sun's coming up.
Nathanael:	Maybe we should try closer to shore.
Disciple 1:	I'm tired of trying.
Disciple 2:	So am I. Let's go home. (*They turn their chairs around, face front and row. Jesus enters down side aisle, stands center front and calls.*)
Jesus:	Friends, haven't you any fish?
Thomas:	(*Calls back.*) No. Not even one.
Jesus:	Throw your net on the right side of the boat and you will find some. (*Disciples look at each other, shrug, and try once more. Peter pulls up the net of fish and others simulate pulling in a large number of fish. They exclaim and make excited remarks as the catch increases.*)
Disciple 1:	One hundred and fifty three large fish. Can you believe this.
Thomas:	Very strange. (*John recognizes Jesus, stands up and cries out.*).

135

John:	It's the Lord!. It's the Lord! (*Peter shouts for joy, grabs his cloak and jumps into the lake. He swims to shore and others follow in the boat.*)
Peter:	Oh, my Lord.
Jesus:	Peace be with you, Peter. Bring some of the fish you have just caught. (*Peter runs to the boat and drags the net ashore. Hands the fish to Jesus who lays them in the skillet. Others come forward, each carrying their chair and fishing gear. They place these against the wall.*)
John:	Shalom, my Lord. (*All others murmur the greeting.*)
Jesus:	Shalom, my friends. Now come and have breakfast. (*As they simulate eating, they sing, stanzas 1-5 of "It's Jesus Christ, Hallelujah!" (EXHIBIT A-3). Peter stands and motions the worshipers to join in.*)

2. After the song, Jesus rises, stands behind the table and the disciples join him on either side. Jesus speaks to the worshipers.

Jesus:	Three years ago, I told Simon Peter, "You are a fisherman, but as of this day, I want you to be my follower. From now on you will catch people for God." Peter became my disciple. Soon there were twelve of them.
	This morning we shared another story. About fishing. About seven disciples, Peter. James, John, Thomas, Nathanael and two others, who recognized me as the risen Lord. About eating together. About the joy of being together—Master and disciples, Jesus and followers, the Son of God and those who believe. (*Ask the worshipers to join him in reading John 3:16 in unison.*)
	But now it's your turn. What do you have in your hands? Fish? You too have been on the Sea of Galilee with the disciples. The water surrounds you (*point to the blue streamers*). Now come to dry land. You too are my followers. Be my guests this morning. I invite you. Bring your fish ashore. Lay them on the table here. Come and have breakfast. (*Worshipers come forward. Jesus and the disciples serve donuts and juice. Ask each one to return to their seats to eat and drink.*)

3. When all have eaten, Jesus steps forward once more, asks the worshipers to rise, and speaks the Numbers 6:24-25 benediction blessing.

Jesus:	The Lord bless you and keep you; the Lord make his face shine upon you and be gracious to you; the Lord turn his face toward you and give you peace. Amen.

As Jesus exits down center aisle, the seven disciples step forward, form a semi circle and lead the worshipers in singing, "Praise God." (EXHIBIT A-5)

B. INTERGENERATIONAL ACTIVITIES

Walking Towards Pentecost Activities

Participants in this center make or engage in one of these activities.

1. **FISHERMEN MAZE.** The maze includes the names of Jesus and the seven disciples in John 21. Two disciples are not identified in the text, but names for them have been selected from the disciple list in Matthew 10:2-4. Make copies of the maze. (You may prefer to enlarge it.) Lay the copies and pencils on the table. Make a sign, FISHERMEN MAZE, and set on the table. The answers are: Thomas, Andrew, Simon Peter, Nathanael, John, James, Bartholomew, Jesus.

FISHERMAN MAZE

1. Find the seven disciples who were fishing.

2. Find the name of the risen Lord.

3. The names may appear horizontally, vertically or diagonally.

4. Circle the words you find. Here is your first clue: Find and read John 21:1-3.

Two of the disciples are not named but names have been selected for them from Jesus' other followers. Here is your second clue: Read Matthew 10:2-4.

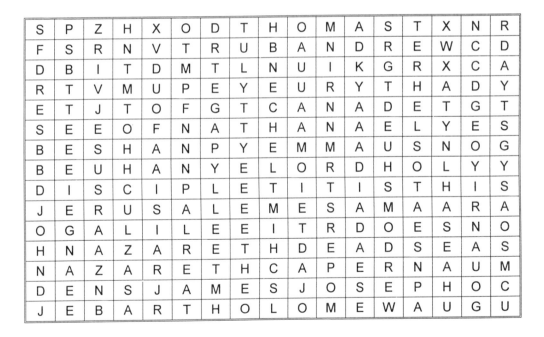

S	P	Z	H	X	O	D	T	H	O	M	A	S	T	X	N	R
F	S	R	N	V	T	R	U	B	A	N	D	R	E	W	C	D
D	B	I	T	D	M	T	L	N	U	I	K	G	R	X	C	A
R	T	V	M	U	P	E	Y	E	U	R	Y	T	H	A	D	Y
E	T	J	T	O	F	G	T	C	A	N	A	D	E	T	G	T
S	E	E	O	F	N	A	T	H	A	N	A	E	L	Y	E	S
B	E	S	H	A	N	P	Y	E	M	M	A	U	S	N	O	G
B	E	U	H	A	N	Y	E	L	O	R	D	H	O	L	Y	Y
D	I	S	C	I	P	L	E	T	I	T	I	S	T	H	I	S
J	E	R	U	S	A	L	E	M	E	S	A	M	A	A	R	A
O	G	A	L	I	L	E	E	I	T	R	D	O	E	S	N	O
H	N	A	Z	A	R	E	T	H	D	E	A	D	S	E	A	S
N	A	Z	A	R	E	T	H	C	A	P	E	R	N	A	U	M
D	E	N	S	J	A	M	E	S	J	O	S	E	P	H	O	C
J	E	B	A	R	T	H	O	L	O	M	E	W	A	U	G	U

2. FEED MY LAMBS. Make copies of the lamb pattern below. Cut posterboard into 16" x 11" sheets. Lay these and cotton balls, scissors and glue on the table. Provide small black buttons or beads for eyes. Make a lamb for demonstration purposes. Use the pattern below:

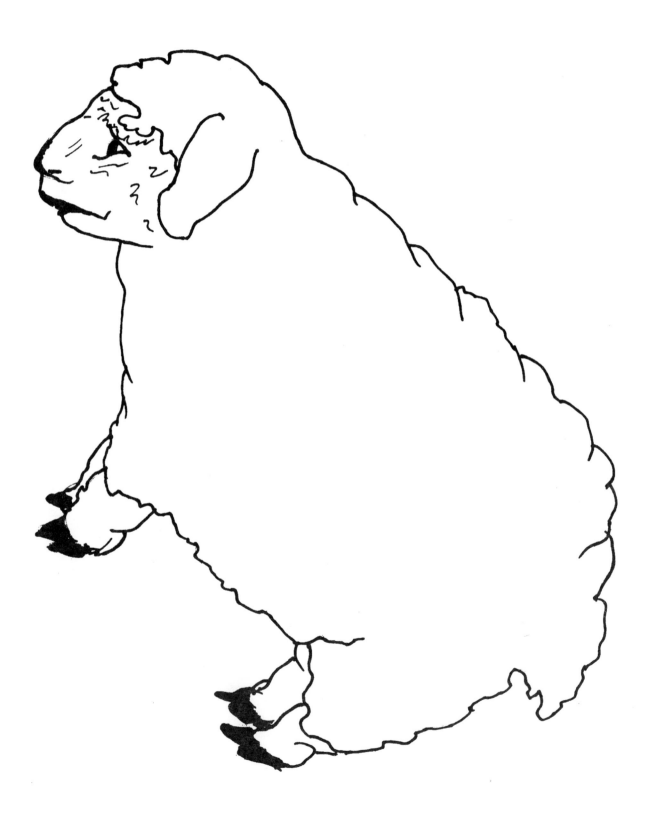

❑ Write these instructions on a stand-up poster and set on the table.

FEED MY LAMBS

Jesus said, "Feed my lambs," to Peter. He meant, "Let all little children know that God loves them." Make a lamb and think, "God loves me."

◆ Fold the large posterboard sheet in half.

◆ Glue the lamb picture on one side, its back on the middle fold.

◆ Cut out the lamb on both sides of the posterboard (*don't cut on the fold*).

◆ Glue cotton balls to the lamb on both sides.

◆ Glue on buttons or beads for eyes.

◆ Lift up the lamb and help it stand.

Holy Spirit Banner Center

Instructions for the Holy Spirit Banner are found in Exhibit C-1. Supply cardboard flame patterns of various sizes, scissors, and on this sixth Sunday provide a checked maroon material.

Pentecost Tree Decoration Center

❑ Each Sunday participants make and hang ornaments that reflect the theme of the 50 days from Easter to Pentecost.

❑ **LAMBS OF GOD**: John 21:1-17 incorporates two events, the disciple-master breakfast and Peter's love test by Jesus. The symbol selected is that of a lamb or sheep. Enlarge and cut out the pattern below. Make several more.

❑ Lay patterns, posterboard, miniature marshmallows and chocolate chips on the table. <u>Option</u>: Make edible ornaments. Bake lamb shaped sugar cookies in advance. Before baking, insert a 1/2" paper straw in middle of backs so they can be hung. Pull straws out right after baking. Hang with narrow ribbon. Use frosting to adhere the marshmallows. Write these instructions on a poster (*adapt, if you use the option*).

LAMBS OF GOD

♦ The sheep or lambs remind us that Jesus is the good Shepherd who takes care of us.

♦ Lay the sheep pattern on poster board.

♦ Trace around the sheep and cut it out.

♦ Glue marshmallows on the sheep to make it look fluffy.

♦ Add a chocolate chip for eye.

♦ Hang it on the Pentecost tree.

Easter-Pentecost Discussion Group *(Use all or select.)*

Search the Scripture.

❏ Read John 21:1-17

❏ What is different about the location of this appearance?

❏ Describe Jesus' role in this incident.

❏ Compare Peter's three affirmations to the three earlier denials (John 18:15-27). What has happened here?

Discuss the Questions.

❏ This Sea of Galilee story concludes a three-year cycle for Peter, beginning with the call to discipleship (Matthew 4:18-20) at the Sea, to the commission for ministry (John 21:15-17) beside the Sea. There has been much 'water over the bridge' in between. Talk about Peter's experiences. Reflect on your last three years. How are your experiences similar or different from Peter's?

❏ Love not duty is the motivating force for the Christian follower, according to Jesus' words to Peter (Matthew 22:37-40). Do you agree or disagree. Why or why not?

Engage in Group Response.

Materials: construction paper, scissors.

❏ Discuss the three Greek words for love; 1. eros—human, sexual love. 2. philia—love for a friend. 3. agape—self-giving love. Reflect on your understanding of love. Cut a paper symbol to represent your understanding. Share and discuss. Sing one of the following: "They Will Know We Are Christians By Our Love," "For God So Loved Us," or "How Great Thou Art."

Refreshment Table

Cover a table with a maroon cloth to match the colors of the flames in the banner. (See Holy Spirit Banner Center.) You have a choice of two types of refreshments, each related to the theme of the morning or more generally with the Easter-Pentecost season.

A. Tuna Ribbon Sandwiches. Mix tuna with minced celery and onion. Add mayonnaise to make a spreading consistency. Spread on slices of bread, stacking them about 6 slices high. With a sharp knife, remove crusts. Wrap in plastic wrap and chill. Cut into thin slices.

B. Swiss-Volhynian Poppy Seed Roll.
- *2 pkg fast rising yeast*
- *1/2 cup sugar*
- *1 cup lukewarm milk*
- *1 tsp grated lemon rind*
- *5 to 5 1/2 cups flour*
- *1/2 cup lukewarm water*
- *3 eggs*
- *1/3 cup oil*
- *1 tsp vanilla*

Stir 1 tsp sugar into warm water and add yeast. Let rise 10 minutes.

Beat the eggs and sugar until lemon colored. Add oil, milk, salt, vanilla, and lemon rind. Add the yeast mixture. Slowly add flour, beating after each addition. Add the last of the flour and knead until smooth and elastic. Place in a greased bowl, cover and let rise in a warm place. After 15 minutes, knead it again. Do this two more times. Cut dough in half and form balls. Roll into two large rectangles. Spread with the poppy seed filling. Roll up as for jelly roll. Seal ends and side. Brush top with egg yolk beaten with 2 tsp water. Let rise until double in bulk. Bake at 350 about 35-45 minutes.

POPPY SEED FILLING
- *1/4 cup butter*
- *2 Tbsp whipping cream*
- *1 egg white*
- *1/2 cup sugar*
- *1 cup poppy seed*
- *2/3 cup crushed almonds or pecans*

Grind poppy seed in blender. Beat butter, sugar and cream. Add poppy seed, and nuts. Whip egg white and fold into mixture. Spoon onto dough, spread, and roll up.

The Happy Clown *(optional)*

Jesus is present, dressed as a happy clown, representing the theme each Sunday. On this Sixth Sunday, the clown walks around, mixes with the groups and joyfully serves or assists all ages.

"WITH GREAT JOY!"

Luke John 21:1-14

GETTING READY: Prepare and do the following in advance:

- ❑ Check to make sure the youth or adult taking on the Jesus role earlier is available.

- ❑ Find a sheer curtain or other sheer material to serve as a cloud for the ascension (*Jesus wears it around his neck, under his robe*).

- ❑ Ask the persons who took on the roles of disciples earlier (Fifth Sunday) to resume their parts in this week's skit.

- ❑ Disciples learn the song, "I Have Decided." (EXHIBIT B-3) (Optional: The traditional "I Have Decided to Follow Jesus," Sing and Rejoice. Faith and Life Press. Newton, KS 1979 #39)

- ❑ Contact the two dressed in white (*First Sunday*) to participate.

- ❑ Make a large sign, BETHANY, and post to the left where all can see it.

- ❑ Post the JERUSALEM sign far to the right, where all can see it.

- ❑ Place chairs and a table near the JERUSALEM sign.

- ❑ Place a platter with two loaves of sweetened or raisin bread on the table. (*Set out several additional plates and a sharp knife.*)

- ❑ Place a Bible on the table.

- ❑ Purchase heavy yarn, and paper for signs, to make a GOOD NEWS COLLAGE. Cut 8 large circles, 3 signs and follow directions in EXHIBIT C-3. (*This collage remains in place for next Sunday.*)

- ❑ Check with the quartet or octet to make sure the group is available to sing, "Holy Spirit, Come with Power" (EXHIBIT C-2) today and again next Sunday.

- ❑ Purchase 3"x5" file cards in various colors, cut in half and provide pens or pencils for the worshipers. Pass these out as worshipers enter.

A. THE WORSHIP:

1. The disciples come in from all sides and sit on chairs near the JERUSALEM sign. They sing, "I Have Decided" (EXHIBIT B-3). Jesus enters and sits with them. Looks at each one and speaks. As he talks, he cuts one loaf of bread into slices, then into smaller pieces, and puts them on plates.

Jesus:	It's been forty days since resurrection morning. I've appeared to you at different times and in different places. Many others have seen me; more than 500 in all. (*Disciples gasp.*) My Heavenly Father, has given me this time to be with you. This helps you remember, that I am risen indeed. You must never lose faith, even in hard times, because that is your hope. You too shall rise again.
John:	Master, what are you saying? This sounds like a farewell speech. I feel the way I did, the night we ate the Seder in the upper room.
Thomas:	(*Anxiously.*) You're not going to be crucified again are you? Are they still looking for you?
Peter:	Just let them try (*tough voice*). We'd handle it better this time.
Jesus:	Peter, you are to feed my lambs, my little ones (*indicate the children*). You are to nourish my sheep, the fathers and mothers, the young people and older people. Yours must be the way of love not anger, peace not violence. (*Turns to Thomas.*) No, Thomas, no crucifixion. It is done.
Peter:	(*Interrupts*) But my Lord, you know I love you. I would give my life for you.
Jesus:	Yes Peter, I know. I know.
James:	Are you then ready to establish the Kingdom of Israel as in the time of David? And can we help you lead the nation, Jesus?
Jesus:	I have taught you many times about the kingdom, James. I have told you, my kingdom is not of this earth. I have shown you the ways of God, now it's up to you.
Nathaniel:	Then you are leaving?
Jesus:	Yes. Remember, our talk, the night of the Seder (*Passover*) meal? I said, "I am going to prepare a place for you." Now it's time. But I said it then, and I say it again. You won't be alone. My Holy Spirit will come to teach, guide and comfort you. The Spirit will give you power and courage. And in that Spirit, I will be with you to the end of time. Don't be afraid. (*Passes several plates of bread pieces to the disciples. He holds up the second loaf.*) And now let's break bread together, all of us, once more. (*Jesus breaks the bread, turns to the worshipers and speaks this prayer:*) Dear God, the giver of all good, we thank you for this gift of food. Amen.
Philip:	What are we to do?
Jesus:	Take this bread and share it with all here. (*He looks at the worshipers.*) Every time you eat, you will remember me, you will think of my words, and my great love for you. (*Disciples pass the bread to the worshipers. While doing so, disciples and worshipers sing "Praise God." (EXHIBIT A-5) They stand in a semi-circle around Jesus, looking at him expectantly. Jesus picks up the Bible.*)
Jesus:	Now let us walk to Bethany. It is only a few miles from here.
Bartholomew:	(*to John*) What's at Bethany?

John:	Maybe he wants to visit Mary, Martha and Lazarus. After all, they were his close friends. (*All move to the Bethany sign.*)
Jesus:	This is goodbye, my friends. (*He embraces each one, then opens the Bible and reads Acts 1:4, 8. As he names the locations, he points to each one on the collage, and sweeps his arms around the room when designating the ends of the earth. He hands the Bible to John.*) Now let me bless you, all of you. (*Stretches out his arms, towards disciples and worshipers and cites the Numbers 6:24-26 blessing.*)
Jesus:	The Lord bless you and keep you; the Lord make his face shine upon you and be gracious to you; the Lord turn his face toward you and give you peace. Amen. (*Disciples bow their heads. During the blessing, Jesus pulls the veil over his head and exits down aisle. At "Amen" disciples open their eyes.*)
All in unison:	He's leaving. (*They continue to look after him, motion the worshipers to join them and all sing stanzas 1-3 of "It's Jesus Christ, Hallelujah!" (EXHIBIT A-3) As they sing, the two in white enter down side aisle and address the disciples.*)
Two in white:	Why are you standing here? Looking? This same Jesus who just left, is coming back. Be joyful. Be glad. Go. You have good news to share. (*All except John, exit, arms waving joyfully and walking in a dance-like step that exudes praise. They sing stanzas 5-7 of, "It's Jesus Christ, Hallelujah!"*) (EXHIBIT A-3)

2. John remains center front, smiling, reaches out his arms as an invitation for all to sing along.

John:	(*Reads Luke 24:52.*) Good news. We have good news to share. We have good news. You have good news. (*He invites the worshipers to participate in sharing the good news by writing a good news message on the card. Indicates that the church's address will be placed on the back. On Pentecost Sunday, these notes will be attached to balloons, launched and sent into the world as ambassadors of good news.*)

3. John collects the cards. During this time, the octet or quartet sings, "Holy Spirit, Come With Power." (EXHIBIT A-1). When all is done, John invites the worshipers to stand and all say the Lord's Prayer in unison.

B. INTERGENERATIONAL ACTIVITIES

Walking Towards Pentecost Activities

Participants in this center make or engage in one of these activities.

1. **GOOD NEWS FLOWER CARD.** Jesus' Ascension and pending Pentecost, prepare Christ's followers for the budding and flowering of the church. Provide red paper 8 1/2x11, paper baking cups, large buttons, green construction paper, scissors, glue and marking pens. Make one card and set it on the table for demonstration.

❑ Write these instructions on a stand-up poster and set on the table.

GOOD NEWS FLOWER CARD

◆ Fold a sheet of paper in half.

◆ Cut a stem and leaves from green construction paper.

◆ Glue onto card.

◆ Glue the bottom of one paper baking cup onto top of stem.

◆ Glue the bottom of a second baking cup into the first.

◆ Glue a button into the center of the second cup.

◆ Make cuts to the bottom of each cup, about every third pleat.

◆ Ruffle the cut edges to look like blossoms.

◆ Write GOOD NEWS on the card and a special message inside. Give your card to someone this week.

2. **THIS IS THE CHURCH BANK.** With Ascension, Jesus commissions his followers to carry on his work. They will do this when they are empowered at Pentecost. The church is birthed. Save pint or 1/2 pint milk and cream cartons. Provide cartons, 4' squares of cardboard, green felt, construction paper, glue, sharp knife and scissors. Make a model. Write these instructions on a stand-up poster.

THIS IS THE CHURCH BANK.

◆ Cut sides and roof from construction paper and glue onto carton.

◆ From construction paper cut a front and steeple for the church.

◆ From colored paper cut windows and a front door; glue in place.

◆ Cut and glue green felt onto a cardboard square.

◆ Glue the church bottom onto the center of the felt.

◆ Draw a cross in the steeple and cut a coin slot in the roof.

Holy Spirit Banner Center

Instructions for the Holy Spirit Banner are found in Exhibit C-1. Supply cardboard flame patterns of various sizes, scissors, and on this seventh Sunday provide a white material.

Pentecost Tree Decoration Center.

Each Sunday participants make and hang ornaments that reflect the theme of the 50 days from Easter to Pentecost.

GOOD NEWS CHAIN: A symbol for this story is expressed by a chain of letters spelling GOOD NEWS. This chain is tied to others, until the whole length circles the Pentecost tree like a garland, not unlike the Good News encircling the world. Provide 3" cardboard patterns for the letters, **GOOD NEWS**. Lay these and red construction paper, pencils, scissors, thread and needles on the table. Write these instructions on a poster.

GOOD NEWS CHAIN

Jesus gave the disciples and us, good news to share. Make a chain, and together with others, share the good news.

◆ Draw around the letter patterns on red paper.

◆ The letters should spell GOOD NEWS. Cut out.

◆ Thread a needle and long thread.

◆ Push your needle in and out at the top of the letters.

◆ When finished, tie your chain to someone elses.

◆ When all chains are finished, make one long one.

◆ Drape around the Pentecost tree and rearrange the letters.

Easter-Pentecost Discussion Group *(Use all or select)*

Search the Scripture.

Read Luke 24:50-52, Acts 1:4-11

❏ Compare the two ascension accounts with Mark 16:19-20.

❏ All four gospels present Christ's challenge to spread the good news, but not all are expressed in the same situation or place. Compare the Luke and Acts accounts with Mark 16:14-18, Matthew 28:16-26, John 20:21-23. What is the central theme throughout?

Discuss the Questions.

❑ How and where is the good news shared in today's world by your denomination? Church? Your family? By you? Discuss and share.

❑ Weigh your understanding of the good news against the proclamation of Jesus in Luke 4:18-19. What does Christ's 'wholeness' approach tell you about the nature and meaning of the gospel?

Engage in Group Response.

❑ Ask someone in your congregation who has been involved in a mission or service experience, to share briefly with your group. Recognize that mission is not only 'out there,' it's as integral to faith as yeast is to bread dough. Break and eat bread together, reflect on, and share ways you have shared the good news since Easter morning. Pray the prayer of St. Francis of Assisi, "Lord, make me an instrument of Thy peace."

Refreshment Table

Cover a table with a white cloth to match the colors of the flames in the banner. (See Holy Spirit Banner Center.) You have a choice of two types of refreshments, each related to the theme of the morning or more generally with the Easter Pentecost season.

A. Banana And Peanut Butter Energy Roll. Purchase unsliced bread and slice lengthwise. Trim off all crusts. Spread each slice with peanut butter, lay a banana (cut to size) at one end and roll up as for jelly roll.

Wrap in plastic wrap. Before serving, cut in slices.

B. Almond Bread From Germany.

- 2 pkg fast rising yeast
- 2 eggs
- 1/2 cup shortening
- 1 tsp almond extract
- 5 to 5 1/2 cups flour
- 1/2 cup lukewarm water
- 1/2 cup sugar
- 1 cup lukewarm milk
- 1 1/2 tsp salt
- 12 oz can of almond paste

Stir 1 tsp sugar into warm water and add yeast. Let rise 10 minutes.

Cream shortening and sugar. Add eggs and beat until lemon colored. Add milk, salt and almond extract. Add the yeast mixture. Gradually add flour, beating after each addition. Add the last of the flour and knead until smooth and elastic. Place in a greased bowl, cover and let rise in a warm place. After 15 minutes, knead it again. Do this two more times. Divide dough in half. Divide each half into two pieces, one twice as large as the other. Divide the larger piece into three pieces and roll into three 16 inch ropes. Braid the strips, pinch ends and lay on a greased baking sheet. With side of your hand, press a trench down the middle, and fill with almond paste. Make a similar braid of the smaller piece and lay on top of the larger one. Fasten with toothpicks. Brush with almond paste. Make a second loaf from the other half of dough. Brush both loaves with beaten egg white. Cover lightly and let rise until double in bulk. Bake at 325 for about 45 minutes. Cool and remove toothpicks.

Adapted from: Voth, Norma Jost, *Festive Breads of Easter*. Herald Press, Scottdale, PA, 1980, page 55-56. Used by permission.

The Happy Clown *(optional)*

Jesus is present, dressed as a happy clown, representing the theme each Sunday. On this Seventh Sunday, the clown walks around, wearing a placard that reads, SHARE THE GOOD NEWS. Pantomimes this sharing in various ways, to all ages.

"HALLELUJAH"

Acts 1:12-14, 2:1-14

GETTING READY: Prepare and do the following in advance:

❑ Contact disciples, women, children and youth of all ages, to be part of the Pentecost gathering.

❑ Ask someone with dramatic reading skills, to read the Reader parts and give leadership as indicated.

❑ Assign members of the Pentecost gathering to take on reader roles for: Peter, John, Stephen, Philip. Barnabas, Paul, Mark, Luke.

❑ Rehearse at least once, so that pantomime, song, response and readings fit together smoothly.

❑ Make a HOLY SPIRIT MOBILE. Purchase a large styrofoam circle (used for making wreaths) and spray paint red. Attach a long string to three sections and tie these together (like a hanging plant) about 2' above the center. Lead the remaining string through a hook, front center ceiling (for raising and lowering purposes.)

❑ Cut red cloth flames and hand these to the worshipers as they enter.

❑ Hand out a candle and holder to each worshiping family unit.

❑ Make copies of the prayer, *Come, Holy Spirit, God Of Love,* and hand to worshipers as they arrive.

❑ Place a chair and table, front back, and set the mobile on it.

❑ Place pins, matches and a number of unlit candles on the table.

❑ Inflate a large balloon, hide it near the table and assign a disciple to punch it as indicated.

❑ Print the words, PHOENICIA, CYPRUS, ANTIOCH, ASIA, GREECE and ROME, on the WORLD circles, (GOOD NEWS COLLAGE) attached to the walls (EXHIBIT C-3).

❑ Post the JERUSALEM sign where all can see it.

❑ Check with the quartet or octet to make sure the group is available to sing, "Holy Spirit, Come," (EXHIBIT C-2) today.

❑ Prelude music is optional.

❑ Purchase balloons, fill with helium, and attach long strings.

❑ Spray a fixative on the GOOD NEWS cards (collected last Sunday), punch a hole in each one, stamp your church's address on back, and tie to balloons.

A. THE WORSHIP:

1. Post two followers (any age) at the door and another one at the table. As worshipers enter, one follower hands out red flames. The second follower gives an unlit candle to each family unit and directs them to the table, front center. When they come to the table, the third follower instructs them how to pin their flames to the HOLY SPIRIT MOBILE (flames hang down). *(Prelude music may be played during this time.)*

2. The 'gathered community,' seated with the worshipers, moves to the front, coming down different aisles. They form a large semi-circle, kneel, fold their hands, close eyes and lift faces in prayer. *(During this time, the follower at the table, quietly raises the HOLY SPIRIT MOBILE. He or she remains at the table but in a prayer position).* As the last ones come forward, the octet sings stanza 1 of, "Holy Spirit, Come." (EXHIBIT C-2)

Reader: *(Reads Luke 24:50-52, with the following word changes.)* When Jesus had led them out to the vicinity of Bethany, he lifted up his hands and blessed them. While he was blessing them, he left them and was taken up into heaven. Then they worshiped him and returned to Jerusalem with great joy. *(Reads Acts 1:13-14. When finished, says the following.)* We are all together in prayer, this Pentecost Sunday. Waiting, waiting. Waiting for the promised power. Waiting for the guide, the counselor, the presence of Jesus Christ, through his Holy Spirit.

3. The Reader invites the worshipers to kneel, and with the 'gathered community,' pray the unison prayer,

COME, HOLY SPIRIT

Come, Holy spirit, God of Love

And give us power from above,

Through Jesus Christ, your only son.

Grant us a love that makes us one.

You are the truth, the life , the way.

Help us to share that news today.

Good news. Good news. Good news, we say.

With joyfilled hearts we kneel and pray.

Come Holy Spirit from above

And fill us with the God of love. Amen.

4. All remain in a prayer position as the octet sings the stanza 2 of "Holy Spirit, Come." (EXHIBIT C-2) After the singing, all rise. Worshipers are seated.

5. *(Reader comes forward)*

Reader: Reads Acts 2:1-4. *(During the reading, the follower lowers the HOLY SPIRIT MOBILE. As the reading ends, the follower punctures the balloon. All jump, look up, murmur ecstatically, raise their hands in worship, surprise and joy. They excitedly call out words and phrases like: "Thank you Jesus!" "Praise God." "The Holy Spirit has come." "Jesus' power is here." "I'm not afraid anymore." "I want to tell everybody about Jesus." "I've never felt this happy." "This is the most remarkable day." "Praise the Lord!" Tempo and volume increases.)*

The Reader encourages the worshipers to join in by singing stanzas 5-9 of, "It's Jesus Christ, Halleluiah!"

(EXHIBIT A-3) During the singing, assigned followers light the candles on the table and using some of these, move among the worshipers, lighting all the candles. During stanzas 8-9, all ages of the 'gathered community,' emoting joy and exuberance, take their places with the worshipers. (*The Reader and those participating in the next part remain at front.*)

6. (*The latter take their places as indicated.*)

Reader:	(*Reads Acts 2:14*)
Peter:	(*Moves beside JERUSALEM sign*).Yes that was quite a day! My name is Peter. I was there! I was Jesus' disciple but I used to be a coward. I betrayed Jesus. I was afraid. But God's Spirit gave me courage. I preached on Pentecost day and 3000 people heard the good news and believed in Jesus.
John:	(*Stands beside Peter*). My name is John. I was Jesus' disciple too. After Pentecost, I was glad to tell others about Jesus. Later I wrote the gospel of John so that the whole world could know about him.
Stephen:	(*Stands beside John*). My name is Stephen. My church started at Pentecost and I was one of the helpers. I shared the good news. Some people got angry and stoned me to death. I wasn't afraid.... the Holy Spirit gave me courage!
Philip:	(*Stands near SAMARIA sign.*). My name is Philip. I was one of Jesus' disciples too. Before Pentecost I didn't have enough love and compassion to share the good news with people who were not like me. Now, I wanted to share God's love with everybody, even the people in Samaria.
Barnabas:	(*Stands near ANTIOCH sign.*) My name is Barnabes. Some of us went to Phoenicia, others to the island of Cyprus in the Mediterranean and to the city of Antioch. We shared the good news of Jesus with the Jews. The Greeks started to believe too. They were overjoyed!
Paul:	(*Stands next to the ASIA sign.*) My name is Paul. At first I was against these Jesus followers. Then, I became one of them and God sent me to share the good news all over the world; Asia, Europe, Rome. (*Moves from one sign to the next.*) Many people became Jesus' followers. Churches were started. In the New Testament you can read the letters I wrote to the churches at Rome, Corinth, Ephesus and many more.
Mark:	(*Stands beside Paul at ASIA sign.*) My name is Mark. I was young but I went with Paul. I wrote the gospel of Mark. You know about it!
Luke:	(*Stands beside Mark*). My name is Luke. I'm a doctor and went with Paul. I wrote Luke and Acts; stories about God, Jesus and the Holy Spirit.
Unison:	This is how the church started. Many shared the good news and many share it today. The church grew and is growing. (*All hold their positions while the octet sings,*

stanza 3 of, "Holy Spirit. Come." Paul moves forward and stands beside Reader.)

Paul: (*Speaks to worshipers.*) Today we celebrate Pentecost, the birthday of the church. Would you like to share the good news on this Pentecost Sunday?" (*The Reader explains how all will participate in a balloon launch with a good news message attached. Asks worshipers to stand for the closing prayer benediction from Numbers 6:24-26.*)

The Lord bless you and keep you; the Lord make his face shine upon you and be gracious to you; the Lord turn his face toward you and give you peace. Amen. (*All move to the door, where they receive balloons and move to the planned outdoor site. After the balloon launch all shout, "Hallelujah!" in unison before going to the fellowship hall*).

B. INTERGENERATIONAL ACTIVITIES.

If possible, extend this Pentecost Sunday fellowship time or select only those activities that you can work in. Plan for a variety of activities at one time. *(The size of the group will determine how this can be best effected.)* While some engage in party activities, others will finish the banner. There may be those who prefer the discussion group. Singing around the tree is a celebrative part of this Sunday. Conclude with refreshments as indicated below.

A Pentecost Party

Suggestions for party plans are found in Part II, Eighth Week under B. BIRTH OF THE CHURCH PARTY. Add other activates or games you would prefer. This time will be concluded with refreshments for all, planned by the group in charge of the Refreshment tables.

Hanging Of The Pentecost Banner

Instructions for the Holy Spirit Banner are found in Exhibit C-1. On this eighth Sunday (Pentecost) provide ready cut red flames, a large white felt dove and the lettering, PENTECOST (or that of your choice). These are quickly adhered to the banner, by the group responsible. If you are hanging the banner in the fellowship hall, plan to do it as part of the "Singing Around the Pentecost Tree event.If it is hung in the sanctuary, arrange with the pastor how this is to be effected. If your congregational worship takes place before your education hour, you will need to complete it earlier and hang it the day before Pentecost. Or plan to incorporate it as part of the worship service (see Part I, Eighth Sunday, THE CONGREGATION AT WORSHIP, under A. THE DRAMA OF WORSHIP.**)**

Singing Around The Pentecost Tree

Make a journey from Easter to Pentecost by gathering around the decorated tree and singing familiar and new hymns. Or sing songs learned during the weeks of walking towards Pentecost. Make the mood celebrative. Accompany the songs with various instruments; string, wind and percussion. Include instruments which children can use such as shakers, triangles, and tambourines.Sing as a group, and also invite in smaller groups who have rehearsed songs for the occasion. Celebrate with music and song.

The songs selected from this book are: "It's Jesus Christ, Hallelujah!" (EXHIBIT A-3), "Praise God and Celebrate the Son" (Exhibit A-5), "Holy Spirit, Come With Power," and "I Have Decided." Other hymns you may want to consider are the following from <u>Hymnal,</u>

a Worship Book (Elgin, IL: Brethren Press; Newton, KS: Faith and Life Press; Scottdale, PA: Mennonite Publishing House, 1992): "They Crucified My Savior," (African American spiritual) #266; "Christ Has Arisen," (Tanzania melody) #267; "Low in the Grave He Lay," #273; "Lift Your Glad Voices," #275; "Look You Saints," #286; "Away with Our Fears," #292; and "God Send Us the Spirit," (Gonja folk melody) #293. You may have other well known or favorite hymns for the Easter-Pentecost season or someone in your congregation may write songs for the occasion.

Easter-Pentecost Discussion Group (*Use all or select.*)

Search the Scripture.

Read Acts 1:12-14, 2:1-14

❑ What is the role of prayer and community in this passage?

❑ Describe the Pentecost event in your own words.

Discuss the Questions.

❑ What is the symbolic meaning of the wind, flames and ecstasy in this passage? How did the waiting and the prayer, prepare those gathered for this intense experience? Share times where group prayer and searching of the scriptures led you to feel your heart 'burning within you' (Luke 24:32). How did this affect your life?

❑ The Greek word for power is 'dunamias', the root of our word dynamite. Jesus sees power of the Spirit (Acts 1:8) as a prerequisite to effective witness. How do you experience the Spirit's 'dynamite' in your life?

Engage in Group Response.

Materials: a six-inch circle with the words "Jesus Christ," printed on it, construction paper, scissors.

❑ Each group member cuts an 11" flame from the paper. Think of a verb or adjective that best describes your understanding and/or experience of the Holy Spirit at work in your life. Write it on the flame. Lay the circle on the floor and all lay their flames around it like flower petals. This flower, with its outstretched petals, is a symbol of believers, reaching out and representing the center, Christ in the world. Sing or read in unison, the words of the hymn, "Holy Spirit, Come with Power." (EXHIBIT C-2)

Refreshment Table

Cover a table with a red cloth to match the colors of the flames in the banner and the Pentecost color. (See Holy Spirit Banner Center.) Only one option this Sunday.

Pentecost Cake. Make a number of round layer cakes depending on size of your group, using white cake mixes. Decorate with red candies (*the color of Pentecost.*) Set the cakes in a circle and with red frosting write a word of the birthday greeting on each cake to represent the unity of the church scattered throughout the world. Write one word on each cake: HAPPY BIRTH DAY TO THE CHURCH. If you have more cakes, you may want to add the date, year or any other message. If you have fewer, you could use 'birthday' as one word. Insert three circles of candles on each cake, to get a flame effect when they're all lit. Serve red punch. At the scheduled time, the cake bearers walk in with the lit cakes, singing (to the tune of Happy Birthday):

Happy birthday, dear church,
Happy birthday, dear church.
Happy birthday, happy birthday.
Happy birthday, dear church.

(*You may want to add other words or stanzas.*) All ages gather around. Sing it two more times. If you used instruments earlier, they could chime in. Call up individuals representing different age groups in the church, to blow them out. Serve with punch. This is the conclusion of your Pentecost celebration. Rejoice! May the Spirits' power rest upon you. Amen.

The Happy Clown *(optional)*

Jesus is present, dressed as a happy clown, representing the theme each Sunday. On this Eighth Sunday, the clown dances and skips around, and joyfully passes out red flames from foil gift wrap to all ages. (These may be added to the Pentecost tree.)

EXHIBIT C-1

HOLY SPIRIT BANNER

1. Cut cardboard flame patterns of different sizes. (Smaller sizes if they are making individual banners.)

2. Purchase the colored materials needed for each Sunday (coordinate with Refreshment Table).

3. Determine the length of banner and buy felt. (If making individual banners, decide on size and number.)

4. Purchase dowels for the banner(s).

5. Sew a 1-inch hem at the top for the dowel.

6. Purchase and add fringes at the bottom (optional).

7. Pencil in an area on banner (banners), where flames are to be contained.

8. Provide glue and allow participants to glue these on in any way.

9. Cut a large dove to glue above the mass of flames when the banner is done.

10. Decide what kind of words you wish to have on the banner (banners), and provide lettering guides. Add to the banner (banners).

EXHIBIT C-2

HOLY SPIRIT, COME WITH POWER

Anne N. Rupp

Anne N, Rupp

Moderately fast with strong beat

1 Ho- ly Spir-it, come with pow-er, breathe in- to our ach- ing night.
2 Ho- ly Spir-it, come with fi- re, burn us with your pres-ence new.
3 Ho- ly Spir-it, bring your mes-sage, burn and breathe each word a- new

We ex- pect you this glad ho- ur, wait-ing for your strength and light.
Let us as one might-y cho- ir sing our hymns of praise to you.
deep in- to our tir- ed liv- ing till we strive your work to do.

We are fear-ful, we are ail-ing, we are weak and self- ish too.
Burn a- way our wast- ed sad-ness and en- flame us with your love.
Teach us love and trust-ing kind-ess, lend our hands to those who hurt.

Break up- on your con- gre- ga- tion, give us vig- or life a- new.
Burst up- on your con- gre- ga- tion, give us glad- ness from a- bove.
Breathe up- on your con- gre- ga- tion and in-spire us with your word.

This melody, written in a rhythmic $\frac{2}{4}$ time, exudes the joy of the Pentecost season. It lends itself to clapping, movement or choreography. An alternative tune is found in Part I of this book.

EXHIBIT C-3

GOOD NEWS COLLAGE

This collage, which adheres to the wall, encircles the room. It symbolizes the spread of the gospel from Jerusalem and other areas in the Holy Land, to the regions far beyond; Asia Minor, Greece and Rome. Some parts of the collage remain undesignated, to remind us that we too are recipients of that Good News, which has spread throughout the world.

From heavy paper cut 8 large circles and 3 signs. The dimensions will need to be judged in terms of the size of your room. The print should be legible from any part of the room. Punch holes in signs and circles as indicated below and fasten the yarn. When finished, the final length of yarn is attached to the right side of the Jerusalem sign, creating a full circle.

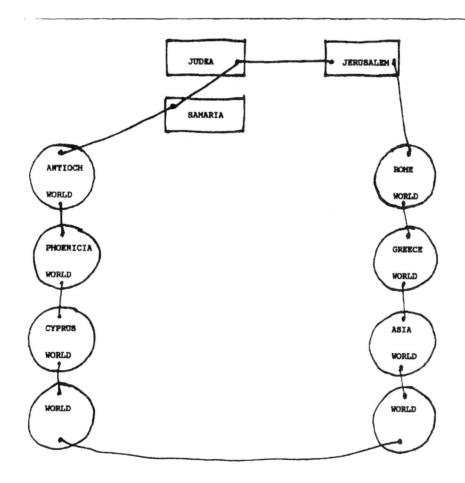